The Jesus Walk

The Road to Healing Body and Soul

by

Patricia A. McLaughlin

PAULIST PRESS
New York/Mahwah, N.J.

Excerpts from THE JERUSALEM BIBLE, Copyright © 1966 by Darton, Longman & Todd, Ltd. and Doubleday, a division of Bantam Doubleday Dell Publishing Group, Inc. Reprinted by permission. Portions of the material on pages 7–13 and 67–68 appeared in the author's article "Great Is His Faithfulness" (SCRC Vision, Vol. XIII, No. 1, January 1986, published by the Southern California Renewal Communities, 2810 Artesia Blvd., Redondo Beach, CA 90278-0389).

The author gratefully acknowledges permission granted by Jean Vanier, Father Jim O'Donnell, and John F. Winters to quote from their material presented at Blessed Are You, a Faith and Sharing Retreat given at the University of San Diego, June 24-29, 1990.

Book design by Theresa M. Sparacio.

Cover design by Cindy Dunne.

Back cover photo by Stephen Ryan Photographics.

Copyright © 1997 by Patricia A. McLaughlin

Library of Congress Cataloging-in-Publication Data

McLaughlin, Patricia A., 1933–
    The Jesus walk : the road to healing body and soul / Patricia A. McLaughlin.
        p. cm.
    Includes bibliographical references.
    ISBN 0-8091-3732-1 (alk. paper)
    1. Jesus Christ—Example. 2. Spiritual healing. 3. McLaughlin, Patricia A., 1933–   . I. Title
BT304.2.M35 1997
248.8'6—dc21   97-20357
                                                                         CIP

Published by Paulist Press
997 Macarthur Boulevard
Mahwah, New Jersey 07430

Printed and bound in the United States of America

Contents

A NOTE TO THE READER 1

1. JESUS WANTS TO WALK WITH YOU 5
   The healing touch of Jesus 6
   Spiritual cancer creates holes in the soul 7
   The roots of illness go deep 8
   Anger with God robs us of his comfort 9
   Miracles are a gift from God 11
   You will come to know the Lord 15

2. THE MYSTERY OF GOD 17
   God is always faithful 17
   Faith is the keystone of healing 18
   Seeing clearly in the dark 19
   The radical way of Jesus 21
   Experiencing the Trinity 22
   Love, reconciliation, and peace 25

3. WONDERFUL YOU 27
   Jesus heals the past as well as the present 29
   The human desire to avoid pain 30
   We need each other 31
   Listening with the heart 32
   An invitation from Jesus 34
   Hidden treasure 35

4. THE LANGUAGE OF LOVE 37
   How can I be perfect? 39
   Prayer reshapes your heart 40
   Reinvent your prayer life 41
   Resting in his presence 43
   Dancing on hot coals 45
   The song in your heart 47

5. JESUS LAUGHED! 49
   What did Jesus laugh about? 50
   Laughter is good medicine 51
   Learn to laugh at yourself 52
   Laughter can be holy 54
   Joy counterbalances sorrow 55
   Jesus wants you to be whole as well as holy 59

6. CHRIST AT THE CENTER 61
   You will become a new creation 62
   Mary shows us how to carry Jesus in the world 63
   Mary was Christ-centered 64
   The empowerment of the Holy Spirit 65
   Jesus wants to empower you 67
   Becoming Christ-centered 70

7. JUST SAY YES! 72
   The Holy Spirit renews God's people 73
   The call to Christian community 75
   Jesus ministers through you 76
   The Spirit is a gentle teacher 77
   Openness to God's Spirit 79
   Changing roadblocks into building blocks 81

8. WHAT WOULD JESUS SAY? 83
   Jesus was a servant leader 84
   Jesus' radical challenge of love 84
   Where are you in this picture? 87
   You need someone you can trust 88
   What is Jesus asking of us? 89
   Reassessing your values 91

9. COME TO THE VINEYARD 93
   Help wanted in the vineyard! Dedication required 94
   Are you willing to labor in the vineyard? 95
   Your thorn is a cross to embrace 96
   God's hidden agenda 97
   The Vinedresser is generous 99
   Come with open hearts and hands 102

10. SEE HOW MUCH HE LOVES YOU 104
   Your listening heart 104
   Offer praise and thanksgiving 105
   Pray with faith, expectation, and discernment 106
   The abiding presence of the Holy Spirit 108
   Using all of the gifts 110
   The importance of nurturing a healing 111
   Jesus prays with you 113

11. THE LIGHT OF CHRIST OVERCOMES DARKNESS ... 115
   Be guided by the wisdom of the Holy Spirit 116
   How Jesus uses you to bring about healing 117
   The key that opens dungeon doors 119
   Jesus frees hidden memories 120
   Jesus, the light of truth who sets us free 122
   Illumination brings transformation 125

12. JESUS HEALS THE BROKENHEARTED 127
   Your inner child has needs too 128
   The ancient path within 129
   Excavation in progress! White gloves required 130
   Honoring and consecrating the sacred site 131
   Deep inner healing is a process 132
   Jesus makes us functional 135

13. ALLOWING GOD TO BE GOD 137
   Healing is God's business; praying is ours 137
   Taking down the wall brick by brick 138
   Attitudes and behaviors that undermine healing 139
   The power of Christ expels evil 140
   Restoring the family tree to health 142
   Jesus opens prison doors and frees captives 147

14. JESUS IS THE RESURRECTION AND THE LIFE 149
   Accept the wisdom of the Healer 149
   Your will be done, Lord 150
   Understanding special needs of the dying 151
   Healing with the Bread of Life and ordinary love 153
   There is a time for letting go 155
   The homecoming for which the soul was created 158

15. HEALING THE WORLD 160
    Be little! 160
    Start an avalanche of healing 161
    Healing disunity in God's family 162
    Jesus and children, our hope for the future 162
    You can heal the world! 164
    Well done, little one! 167

NOTES 168

SUGGESTED READING 172

RESOURCES 174

DEDICATION

To my husband Rex, with love.

*To Jesus, my best friend,
praise and thanksgiving for
inviting me to walk with him.*

*To those who read this book,
may you grow in love for Jesus
as you walk with him. You are
all remembered in my prayers.*

ACKNOWLEDGEMENTS

This book could not have been written without the help and involvement of very special people. I extend my heartfelt thanks and gratitude to all who have been involved in my healing; to my family and friends for their love and prayers; and to my editor, Lawrence Boadt, C.S.P, for his sensitive advice and encouragement. Thanks also to Karen Scialabba for her support and enthusiasm, and to everyone at Paulist Press for their talents and contributions.

There is an appointed time for everything,
And a time for every affair under the heavens.
A time to be born, a time to die;
A time to plant, and a time to uproot the plant.
A time to kill, and a time to heal.

Ecclesiastes 3:1–3

A NOTE TO THE READER

*E*very year in the United States, more than a million people are stricken with cancer, and more than half a million people die from the disease. In spite of the ongoing advances in research and medicine, these are grim statistics.[1] Spiritual cancer is even more destructive. It eats holes in the soul and leaves an overwhelming sense of emptiness.

People suffer from spiritual sickness in many different ways. Symptoms can include apathy, anger, disappointment, agnosticism, friction, boredom, denial, and busyness. Spiritual cancer causes people to search for a way to satisfy their deep inner longing. Many look in all the wrong places without filling their empty souls. The world cannot fill their emptiness because separation from God is the underlying problem.

People who need healing for emotional hurts and physical ailments frequently have spiritual wounds as well. Recently, prayer has been added to the list of curatives called "alternative medicine" as researchers document cures, remissions, and miracles attributed to prayer.

Healing has been a concern of the Church since its inception. In dramatic contrast to the Old Testament emphasis on the righteousness of God who continually disciplined an unruly people, Jesus spoke to the uniqueness and importance of the individual. It was through his healing ministry that he revealed the compassion and mercy of his Father. A worldwide movement of the Holy Spirit in the 20th century has given the ministry of healing greater prominence and visibility. This is particularly evident in charismatic churches and communities.

Like many who long for peace, I ventured into the charismatic renewal in a state of brokenness. Even though my spirit had been crippled for years, it was not until my body was ravaged by an incurable physical cancer that I finally took action to

1

heal my wounded soul. In my desperation, I sought help from Catholics who recognized the power of the Holy Spirit.

Within one short month, through the loving touch of Jesus, I was healed both spiritually and physically. Then I received a deep inner healing. God accomplished my healing *through* people. It was through their love and compassion, and through their willingness to listen, to love me, and to pray for me, that I heard Jesus saying, "I want to help you. I want to ease your burdens."

Healing is as accessible to each of us as Jesus is. Jesus is the healer. It is his power, not ours, which enables us to heal others. He uses the listening hearts, human hands, and the prayers of ordinary people to heal.

Since Jesus often effects his healing through the ministrations of medical professionals, it is a grave mistake to discontinue medical treatment while awaiting a miracle. Health specialists frequently pray for their patients, and furthermore, the doctor recognizes with certainty that a person has been healed.

As Jesus continued to lead me, I learned to pray creatively and spontaneously in my own words. I discovered a new hunger for Scripture. At charismatic prayer meetings, I experienced the power of the Holy Spirit, as I learned to use gifts that had remained unwrapped since my youth.

Jesus gave me a gift of praying for healing in others. While some of their stories are shared in this book, fictitious names have been used to protect the privacy of those I have prayed for.

As I continued to step out in faith, I had to overcome a lot of prejudices before I realized that being charismatic is not about hugging, or praying in tongues, or saying "Praise the Lord!" It is about growing into a deep personal relationship with Jesus. It means accepting the gifts of the Holy Spirit. It involves living a life that praises and gives thanks to God not only in thoughts and words, but also through actions.

Prior to my cancer, I would have laughed at any suggestion that I would pray for miracles. However, in my new relationship with Jesus, I felt a strong desire to serve him. New gifts unfolded and I answered a call to organize and lead a charismatic prayer group.

Just when we begin to feel comfortable in our relationship with God, he takes us further. At a retreat in June 1990, Jean Vanier disturbed my tranquility with his challenge to live more fully the gospel message. This remarkable man opened my eyes and my heart to the *little ones* of Jesus.

The message of Jean Vanier is the message of Jesus. We are called to *be*—to be for and with people, to love them as Jesus does, to share their pain, to pray for them. We are called to *be Jesus* by allowing his light to shine through our faces, our words, and our actions.

In this fractured world we are called to *see Jesus* in the broken and poor of this world. Jesus wants us to become like children in our simplicity and love. Vanier said that we meet Jesus in our own brokenness, and in the lonely, the poor, the broken, and the discards of our society. Jesus wants us to move from textbook spirituality to love.

Jesus became bread for us, broken and blessed, so that we might be nourished. He wants to bless and transform our brokenness. Jesus calls us to live the Beatitudes, to be his healing presence in the world, just as that prayer community was for me. He uses the listening hearts, human hands, and the prayers of ordinary people to heal.

Jesus wants you to be present to the *little ones* he claims as his own. He wants you to walk with him through a troubled world, allowing his light to shine through you on those who long for his peace. Jesus is inviting workers to join him in the vineyard.

As you read this book, you are encouraged to use your Bible. By immersing yourself in the Word of God, you will grow closer to the Source of healing. My prayer is that you will know the fullness of the Father's love and that you will be touched and healed in the depths of your being. I pray that Jesus will become your best friend and that his Spirit blesses you in every way. Furthermore, I pray that you will respond to the call for workers in the vineyard.

Patricia A. McLaughlin
The Feast of Our Lady of Lourdes
February 11, 1997

1. Jesus Wants to Walk with You

"Let us make man in our own image...."
(Gn 1:26)

Each morning when I awake, my gaze falls upon a picture of the Laughing Christ. His head is thrown back in merriment and his face radiates joy, reminding me to refrain from taking myself too seriously. Jesus gently teaches me to recreate the wounded child within me. He encourages me to trust in the love of his Father and he sends his Holy Spirit to renew and guide me as I walk the Jesus walk.

Jesus wants to walk more closely with you. His Father's plan for your life is wonderful and unique. Fulfillment of his plan, however, depends upon your cooperation. When you willingly accept divine guidance, he will direct your life in ways you never imagined possible.

You are not an accident that just happened. You were planned by the Father and conceived through the miracle of Divine Love. He created you in his own image, breathing his very Spirit into the infinitesimal beginnings that started your life. (Gn 1:26–27) We are all created to exemplify God's beauty and perfection, but our lives develop along different storylines.

Think of yourself as a garment fashioned from fabric woven on God's loom. The many-colored threads woven in the warp and woof of his foundation give to each life a different pattern. While your life began with fabric unique to you alone, it also was shaped by many outside influences to become the garment you currently wear. Both the circumstances of your birth and the events of your life give your garment or story a color and shape unlike any other.

Are you comfortable in your garment? Does it fit you well?

Even beautiful designer garments can become shabby and ill-fitting. Has yours been stained and snagged by the effects of evil in the world? Has it been stretched out of shape when wrong choices were made? If your garment is less than beautiful, perhaps it has not always received the loving care it needed.

One of the privileges of being God's creation is that he, as your personal designer, continues to offer you help in refashioning your life. He sent us Jesus to remove the soil and snags from our garments, and Jesus sends his Holy Spirit as our personal consultant. With this help, we can redesign and alter our lives. We can be restored to alignment with God's perfect plan for each of us through the healing touch of Jesus.

> We are God's work of art, created in Christ Jesus to live the good life as from the beginning he had meant us to live it.
> (Eph 2:10)

Through the ongoing process of healing, Jesus strips away the many layers of accumulated pain and fills the empty spaces with his love. Regardless of where you are in your life, there is always healing available. With your cooperation, this process can continue throughout your lifetime. Each day presents new situations and problems which may require healing tomorrow.

THE HEALING TOUCH OF JESUS

> And for anyone who is in Christ, there is a new creation...
> (2 Cor 5:17)

When you are "in" Christ, you are immersed in him and he lives fully in you. He continues to purify you and make you whole. He brings you into the perfection the Father wants for each of his children, so that you shine like the image of God and become his reflection to others in the world.

Our lack of perfection is often manifested by emotional breakdown, spiritual sickness, and physical illness, all of which may be outward symptoms of deeper levels of woundedness. As we learn more about the complexity of the human immune system, we better understand the interrelationship of mind, spirit, emotions, and the body.

In my life, those factors worked together and almost brought about my physical destruction. My story, which illustrates some of the ways that deep inner wounding occurs, may give you fresh insight into your own story. Jesus can touch and heal your life as he has mine.

Jesus healed me. I must have been a tough case because I found myself in drastic circumstances before I could open up to his healing touch. The crisis that proved my turning point was the diagnosis of cancer in an advanced stage.

Cancer describes a group of diseases that are marked by the uncontrolled multiplication and the spread of abnormal body cells. Cancer is perhaps one of the most feared words in our vocabulary, conjuring up images of pain, suffering, and death. A cancerous tumor is called malignant, a word which means evil, injurious, destructive, and harmful.

Scientists continue to search for clues to the prevention of cancer. Discovery of the elusive gene, virus, or other hidden factor which causes militant cells to multiply and declare war on the body may someday result in prevention or a cure.

SPIRITUAL CANCER CREATES HOLES IN THE SOUL

Spiritual cancer is an equally insidious disease. It usually begins in a small way but gradually takes over and attempts to devour the soul. My own spiritual cancer took root when as an overly-sensitive child in a dysfunctional family, I developed a warped perception of God as a punishing deity. If anyone told me then how much God loved me, I didn't believe them.

This misperception deepened when the Sister who prepared me for the reception of Eucharist stunned me with the news that my second grade sins had driven spikes through Jesus' flesh and had pressed cruel thorns into his head. I was too shocked and ashamed to tell my parents what I had done. My perception of God grew darker and my First Communion Day was one of the saddest days of my life.

This distorted concept of God followed me into adulthood.

Stuck in my concept of a grumpy, accusing God, I compensated by clinging to my religion dogmatically. The liturgical renewal of Vatican II brought freshening winds to the church but those same changes caused me to feel even more alienated from God.

Even though our family life centered around the Church, I began making excuses to miss Sunday Mass. Pressured by my husband to attend and "set a good example" for our children, I complied reluctantly but my soul-wound deepened. So painful was my experience of the Eucharist, I frequently left church in tears before the Consecration.

THE ROOTS OF ILLNESS GO DEEP

My anger with God and his Church went underground, stuffed into a dark inner place with my repressed fears, neurotic guilt, and a lot of emotional problems. This bundle of negativity seethed and festered within me, until finally it manifested itself in a physical way.

In 1978, my inner time-bomb exploded. It was a hectic December of shopping, baking, going to kids' concerts, and attending to a crowded social calendar. I smiled and laughed, but inwardly I felt the familiar melancholy and depression I had always felt at Christmas. Childhood traumas in a troubled family had left their ghostly imprint. That year there was an additional hurt—a searing pain in my right breast, an abscess the doctor thought. With Christmas a week away and no time to rest, I took my antibiotics and wished that just once I could enjoy the season.

When the doctor examined me two weeks later, the shocked expression on his face told me more than he realized. My condition was worse. He had erred in his diagnosis and I must see a surgeon the following Monday. He did not use the awful "C" word, but deep inside I knew.

My husband was in Saudi Arabia on an extended business trip and unaware of the seriousness of my situation. I passed a tearful weekend reading about breast cancer and by the time I arrived at the surgeon's office on Monday, I had stoically prepared myself for the "inevitable" mastectomy. So often the very thing we fear most does not happen!

The surgeon gently explained that I appeared to have an inoperable type of breast cancer. Since this type was rare, it was not surprising that it had been misdiagnosed. I also had the flu, so in spite of the urgent need for a biopsy, he decided to wait a few days. I was grateful for the opportunity to alert my husband so that he could return home.

Unlike ordinary breast cancer, my rare type was characterized by distinctive symptoms: pain, redness, heat, swelling, an itchy rash, and raised tracks on the skin marking the trail of cancer cells through the lymph vessels. In addition, there were many lumps of cancer and there was lymph node involvement, further indication that the virulent disease was invasive. The biopsy confirmed the surgeon's diagnosis—advanced inflammatory carcinoma of the breast, a terminal and untreatable cancer. Furthermore, my fast-growing tumor was spreading like wildfire.[2]

ANGER WITH GOD ROBS US OF HIS COMFORT

Initially, I sought comfort by confiding in Mary. Since I was no longer on speaking terms with God, I found the gentle Mother of Jesus more approachable. Each night when I prayed and blessed the site of my cancer with Lourdes water, I asked Mary to speak to her Son on my behalf. I hoped that she would somehow sneak my petitions in through the back door. Meanwhile, a paradoxical situation confronted me. Death was dancing around me but I was angry with God. Yet I needed his forgiveness and his mercy.

In desperation, I went to see Father Ron Exley, S.M., who listened with love and compassion as I made a confession of my entire life. Our prayers together provided balm to my wounded soul. I had expected chastisement for being angry with God. Instead, this charismatic priest affirmed me. He said, "Pat, you are so strong—you make me feel strong! You have a lot of faith! Why you've already accepted this!"

His affirmation became the reality. When I heard his words,

I *felt* strong. With the shedding of my anger, a sense of peace and acceptance filled me. My face shone with radiance and I became positive in my outlook. This dramatic change was noticed by my friends and doctors. Even strangers commented on my positive attitude. For years I had battled negativity, without success. Clearly, this deep inner peace could only come from Jesus.

With this spiritual healing came a powerful release of the Holy Spirit in my life. The old negative self was gone, as though I had stepped out of my cancerous shell and become a new person. The intensity of my joy was even greater than the spiritual pain I had felt before. Such a renewal is called Baptism of the Holy Spirit, in which a person is on fire with the Lord. For the first time in my life, I was aware of the Father's abundant love.

A few days later, an oncologist explained that even though my cancer was terminal and untreatable, I might buy a little time with chemotherapy and radiation treatments. There would be serious illness as the cancer spread. I thought the doctor said I had a year, but without treatment the reality was six weeks. I was happily married, with six children between the ages of thirteen and twenty-two. "I'll take a year," I said, "I have a lot to do!"

My main priority was to deepen my new relationship with God the Father. Meanwhile, Father Ron was expecting a miracle. His bold faith amazed me. Furthermore, he asked me if I would talk about it when it happened. Would I! I told him I would shout it from the rooftops. Every Sunday night, I dragged my family to a charismatic Mass which Father Ron and two associates celebrated for the Newman Club. These were joyful two-hour long celebrations of the liturgy amidst a community that continued to lift my family in prayer.

While some of my children were uncomfortable with my sudden involvement in the charismatic renewal, they went along because they couldn't very well refuse a dying mother. Their uneasiness was understandable considering that I, who had been suspicious of anything charismatic, had raised them. Jesus kept drawing me closer and calling me back to this Christ-centered group where I saw his face reflected all around me.

The Eucharist, which had previously caused my weeping, was now my source of gladness. I loved Jesus and he loved me! I continued to pray for a miraculous cure, but even with so many reasons to live, I couldn't feel sad that God was calling me home. This was described as a win-win situation by my husband, who nevertheless was unable to share my peaceful acceptance of death.

The first chemotherapy treatment was given in two parts, beginning January 18th. By January 30th, my symptoms were worse. There was a new lump, I was very ill with a virus, and my hair was falling out. My time was divided between taking care of my large family, trying to say goodbye to all of my friends before I died, and saving enough strength for the Sunday evening Masses.

By the 5th of February, I was relieved that a suspicious large swelling in the back of my throat had disappeared but I was weak from coughing, there was a worrisome new pain in my shoulder, my daughter was recovering from pneumonia, and one son had bronchitis. Also, my husband had narrowly escaped death. While driving my car on a dark rainslick road, he had slid out of control and tumbled down a thirty-foot embankment. Miraculously, he had walked away from the demolished car unhurt. As it often seems to happen, our trouble was multiplying.

MIRACLES ARE A GIFT FROM GOD

There was no improvement in my cancer symptoms. I told Father John McGregor, S.M., that apparently God planned to teach me patience before he granted my miracle. "Pat, don't you know that you cannot earn a miracle?" he replied. I quickly turned away to hide the tears in my eyes. Much later, when we discussed his comment, Father John explained that he had meant to encourage me. "A miracle does not depend on you," he said kindly, "it is a total gift from God. He has his own reasons for granting it."

On February 11th, Father John concelebrated the Sunday Mass with Father Dennis Steik, S.M. I was surprised when they concluded with a healing service! As the congregation lined up on either side of the chapel, Father Dennis commented that Father John was the one with a healing ministry, adding that he

personally felt discouraged when the cancer patients he prayed
for died.

For just an instant, I considered moving over to Father
John's line for anointing and prayers! Father Dennis assured us,
however, that God always answers our prayers in the most loving way when we ask for healing. Healing might be spiritual or
emotional, rather than physical, and often there is a healing of
relationships before the patient dies.

While some people experienced healing of emotional hurts
that evening, all I felt was love. Five days later, I returned to the
oncologist for my second chemotherapy treatment. The cancer
was gone! The redness and other signs were dramatically reced-
ing but most important, all the lumps of cancer had vanished!
The doctor later confided that this was certainly a miracle
because one chemotherapy treatment could not have reversed
my disease.

In spite of my impatience and the total hopelessness of my
advanced cancer, God healed me. He did this even though I
thought I was in the "wrong" line. He used the prayers of the
priest who had never seen a miracle and had even doubted if he
should continue praying for healing. I received a miracle even
though I had accepted my impending death. None of these
things mattered. A miracle *is* a total gift from God.

Was it just a coincidence that my physical healing occurred
on February 11, 1979, the feast day of Our Lady of Lourdes? I
don't think so. I believe that Mary longs to bring us into relationship with her Son. Since my doctor would not approve a trip to
Lourdes, Mary quietly brought Jesus to me in a way that would
give witness to his love. I had promised to "talk about my miracle" and she must have known I would. Jesus healed my disease
while inviting me into a deeper, more personal relationship with
him.

It is one thing to ask for a miracle and quite another to
receive one. This was the first miracle I had ever witnessed and
the realization that it had actually happened to me was difficult
to accept. At first, there were doubts in my mind that the cancer
was really gone. I was even hesitant to tell people for fear I

would look like a fool if the cancer returned. Then I remembered Father John's earlier advice. A miracle is a gift from God.

I knew I wasn't special, though I certainly felt loved. The miracle was not due to my piety. It was not a reward for knowing which prayers to say. My healing did not occur because a certain famous person prayed over me. In fact, Father Dennis had prefaced his healing prayers by announcing that most of the people he prayed for had cancer, and most of them died! It was clear God had a different plan for me that was hidden in mystery.

Many people want to argue about the validity of healings and miracles. "You never had cancer. The doctor made a mistake." "The illness was all in your mind." "You are only in remission. It doesn't mean you have been cured." "The lab that performed the biopsy wasn't credible." Thus was I challenged by skeptics, but I did not allow them to shake my new and growing trust in the Father's love. When I asked Father John how I should respond to people who disbelieved my miracle, his answer was simple, "Just live long enough to prove it!" I have. The invasive cancer has never returned.

Meanwhile, decisions had to be made about the treatments I had begun. From the little that was written about my rare type of cancer, I knew that it was fatal and invasive. The chemotherapy and radiation therapy which were intended to buy some time might also prevent the tumor from returning. Would I lose the miracle if I continued the treatments? Again, Father John's common sense guided me. "Be obedient to your doctors. God works through them."

Even though I am no longer a stranger to miracles, I have never lost my awe over God's loving response to our prayers. By turning over our lives to his care and allowing him the freedom to shape us, we cooperate in his plan for our lives. What I have learned about healing came out of my own faith crisis and the events that followed it.

When we pray with faith for healing, lives begin to change. I have seen remarkable healings in others. There might be a dramatic change of heart. Troubled relationships are mended. Problems large and small are resolved. God changes what we are unable to change. He heals when doctors cannot.

God surrounded me with good teachers and a prayer community of deep faith when he led me into the ministry of healing. As he uses our listening hearts and our healing hands to achieve his healing touch, we are drawn into partnership with the mystery of God.

> You must give up your old way of life; you must put aside your old self, which gets corrupted by following illusory desires. Your mind must be renewed by a spiritual revolution so that you can put on the new self that has been created in God's way, in the goodness and holiness of the truth. (Eph 4:22–24)

† † †

YOU WILL COME TO KNOW THE LORD

Even though we are made in God's image, you may wonder how you can penetrate the deep mystery of the Creator and really come to know him better. I remember a time when I struggled and searched for ways to improve my relationship with the Lord. The harder I tried, the more difficult it became.

Then I was given a prophecy as I meditated on the words, "You will come to know the Lord." When he spoke to my heart, he convinced me that I had to stop searching and simply be present to him. He would do the rest.

Quit your striving. Take a break from your quest to understand God. Just know and accept that he wants that intimate relationship with you.

Get into a comfortable position in a quiet place and relax. Simply be quiet and allow him to come closer. God will lead you into the deeper relationship you both desire.

A MEDITATION AND PROPHECY

You will come to know the Lord! How will this happen? You must *come* to him, not go seeking him. So he must already be present—here with you now.

You—this is something you must do alone. Like birthing or dying. No one can show you how. It is an individual matter. *You* indicates that you must come alone—stand alone in his presence. How can others come to him? Perhaps they will follow along, wanting to come to him whom they see in *you.*

Will—you *will* come—a command, but also something you must will yourself to do. You will come to know the Lord.

Know—how will you know the Lord? You can only know someone by experiencing them—coming closer and touching—being touched. He knows you. You must reach out to him—he will touch you. Therefore, you must be open to the experience and

15

bring yourself into his presence. As you know him, you two will become one—and others will have a greater opportunity to come to him and to know him.

The means the only one—no other. *Lord*—ruler, master, guide, one above all. The one above all else. You will come to know the Lord.

You will can be a command but it can also be a prophecy. You *will* come to know him, in spite of your laziness, your preoccupation with worldly things, your reluctance to take risks. Why? Because he longs for you to come to him. He has put a longing inside of you that no other creature of the world can satisfy. It is as natural for you to seek God as it is for you to be hungry, to grow weary, to thirst.

You *will* be attracted by his goodness, his comfort, his sweet-ness—just as the nose is attracted to pleasant aromas—and once aroused by this attraction you will hunger and thirst for more of him. You cannot be satisfied with just a taste of the Lord—there is always more, greater depths of love, more dizzying heights of fullness, boundless and endless peace to achieve.

YOU WILL COME TO KNOW THE LORD!

2. The Mystery of God

"...who do you say I am?" (Lk 9:20)

*T*ry as we may, we can never fully explain the mystery surrounding God. We can know about God from Holy Scripture, but faith is the necessary prerequisite for accepting the legitimacy of these inspired writings. Faith is the vehicle by which we relate to God.

When we say a person has faith in God, we refer to the belief in a supreme being, in a creator or first cause for all life. While this belief is intangible and difficult to explain to a nonbeliever, you can more easily describe the effects of your relationship with God. Your personal history of God's love and faithfulness in your life provides a powerful frame of reference for your knowledge of God.

GOD IS ALWAYS FAITHFUL

Now that I have a long experience of God's love in my life, I reflect often on his past mercies. These memories of God's faithfulness bolster my faith and give me hope and comfort when new crises arise. Sacred Scripture is filled with memories and recitations of God's mercy.

In my own life, I have learned that God is different in many ways from your friends and relatives, your co-workers and neighbors. Even someone who loves you very much may hurt you and let you down in ways large and small. God is constant and faithful. He will never forget you. He won't, on a whim, turn his back on you. Even when you turn away from God, he is always there, waiting for your return.

Perhaps someone you love has turned away from God.

Does that mean the death of faith? Through my spiritual healing, I learned that even a faith that appears to be dead may simply be dormant. Have you ever watered the dry and crusty soil
of a drooping houseplant and then watched in amazement as it
straightened its stalk and lifted its leaves?

Neglected faith rebounds similarly when given the light of
Christ and the living water of his teachings. Never underesti-
mate the power of God to reverse a seemingly hopeless fall from
grace. The same God who reformed Saul by knocking him off his
horse can melt the most hardened of hearts.

FAITH IS THE KEYSTONE OF HEALING[3]

Prayers for healing at all levels are predicated on faith in
the promises of Jesus. It helps when the recipients of healing
prayer have strong faith, but the lack of such faith does not limit
God's power to heal. God may heal an agnostic to bring about a
conversion. He may heal a believer to give witness to the ailing
person's medical team.

It was Jesus who told us to pray with faith and to expect
God the Father to hear and answer our prayers. (Mt 7:7–11) Jesus
also told us that he is the way to the heart of the Father. For that
reason, we make our petitions in the name of Jesus.

> I tell you solemnly once again, if two of you on earth agree
> to ask anything at all, it will be granted to you by my Father
> in heaven. For where two or three meet in my name, I shall
> be there with them. (Mt 18:19-20)

Perhaps you feel that your faith is not strong enough to ask
big favors from God. Remember that your faith is in God, not in
your own faith. One obstacle to praying with expectant faith is a
feeling of distance from God. Faith is only the first step in knowing God. There are ways that you can improve your relationship
and draw closer to him.

Ask yourself how you know anyone. You may know them
by hearsay, by reputation, or in a shallow, casual way. You really
begin to know a person when you share life experiences on a

deeper and more personal level, and when you have walked together through both good times and difficulties.

When I first suspected that I had breast cancer, I wanted to know "the enemy." I learned everything I could about the disease. Then, with the diagnosis of a terminal illness, I needed to know the oncologist who would help me in my battle. I learned that my doctor had impressive credentials. He also had a good reputation. My surgeon held him in high esteem, and so did the technician who conducted my bone and liver scans. She said he was a dedicated oncologist who fought hard against cancer, and always with the determination to win.

Knowing my oncologist's reputation gave me comfort because I am a fighter too. During the course of chemotherapy treatments, we became better acquainted. I found him to be modest, humble, and caring. His quiet sense of humor buoyed me. In spite of a heavy caseload, he always found time to listen to my questions and to answer them honestly.

We were a team fighting an irreversible disease. When the cancer suddenly vanished a month later, the oncologist shared my awe over this miracle of healing but he urged me to continue the treatments. Because of the respect I had gained for this man, it was easy to trust him, even though I knew the treatments could have long-term damaging effects on my health. We became good friends as he journeyed with me from terminal illness to wellness.

Just as I grew in friendship with the doctor, so must we grow in relationship with God. We can know about God through his reputation and from the recommendations of others. In order to deepen our relationship, we also need to talk with him, to become comfortable in his presence. We need to walk with him through good times and bad. Finally, we need to develop a deep trust in God.

SEEING CLEARLY IN THE DARK

Since God's ways are mysterious, there may be dark moments when we find it difficult to trust him. At those times, it helps to remember that he hears us and loves us even when he appears to be silent. I recognize now that during times that were difficult in spite of my prayers, I lacked the insight to know where God was leading me. God had a plan but it was different from my plan!

Years ago, my husband and I spent a night on our boat with plans to go sailing the next morning. My husband arose early and went above deck, eager to set sail and leave. When I awoke, I looked up through the hatch above my bunk and saw a very dark cloud. I called out that we'd better not go sailing because of the stormy weather. My husband met my announcement with hearty laughter. "Get up and take a look around!" he said. The sky was a brilliant blue as far as I could see, marred only by one small black cloud that hovered directly above our boat. My window on the world was small, indeed. I had not seen the whole picture.

It is so easy to sabotage God's better plan for lives simply because we don't see the whole picture. We don't find it easy to let go of what we want, but God wants our complete trust. If we seek the easy way, always looking for quick solutions to our difficulties, we miss wonderful opportunities to grow into deeper relationship with God. He wants to give us wonderful gifts, but too often we set limits by telling God what to give us. When we surrender in total faith and trust, he surprises us with his generosity.

Faith is more than a deep-seated belief. It is belief in action. Ideally, faith is the underpinning for every decision we make and for every action we take. The gift of faith comes with companion gifts of hope and charity. Hope is the frame of mind that enables us to look to the future in a positive way. It is an expression of our confidence in the promises of God. We are urged, "Let us keep firm in the hope we profess, because the one who made the promise is faithful." (Heb 10:23) Hope sustains our faith when the path is not clearly illuminated.

Charity is our love for God as shown toward others. Charity is a measurement of our love that can be seen through our actions. St. Paul said that words, gifts, and actions are worthless without love. (1 Cor 13:1–3)

Faith bolstered by hope is fulfilled in charity. When we offer ourselves in the service of the Lord, reaching out in love to bring his healing to others, we step into the gospel and bring the message of Jesus to life. Even when the person we pray for has diminished faith and hope, love can remove barriers and open the door. Once that door is cracked open, Jesus can enter.

THE RADICAL WAY OF JESUS

When Jesus taught about the Father's expectations for us, he urged us to become like little children. (Mt 18:3–4) This challenge to become little or simple is in direct conflict with the message of the world, which urges us to take charge and to get control. Worldly power is equated with your material possessions and the power that you wield. Worldly values say that if you go to the right schools, have a prestigious address, drive an expensive automobile, use the right shampoo and deodorant, and wear clothing with correct labels, you will get ahead of the "others."

Life in the power lane consumes so much of our time, energy, and attention. Yet it leaves us feeling unsatisfied. Filling our lives with power and control is like pouring fuel into a leaky tank. No matter how much we pour into it, the gauge never registers full. Sooner or later, the pursuit of worldly power yields a similar result. We come up feeling empty.

Is it possible to live in the world today and still be little? You can't just get from here to there in one leap. The motivation to live life the Jesus way, the radical way, comes out of knowing him in a deep and personal way. There are steps you can take that will help your relationship with God to grow.

Our triune God—Father, Son, and Holy Spirit—knows us intimately. He knows our hopes and desires, our loves and our fears, our sicknesses and our sorrows. Each one of us must answer to God for our actions. We won't be excused because of our apathy. It won't do any good to say, "I was too busy." At the final judgement, Jesus will not measure our worldly success. He will ask what we did to bring his love and peace into the world. He will ask us how well we loved, how well we answered his gospel call.

EXPERIENCING THE TRINITY

If you haven't experienced the three persons of God in an intimate way, there is still time to learn. You can begin to know them better by immersing yourself in Scripture, the inspired writing of those who recorded his Word. As you read, reflect, meditate, and pray on the Word of God, you will begin to know him better.

Conversation with God should be your goal as you become better acquainted with the Father. When I first learned about my cancer, I worried because I had been angry with God for a long time. A wise young priest told me it was all right to be angry, just as long as I kept up my dialogue with God. As if to confirm this, a friend wrote that I should yell at God with outrage, just as the desert prophets had done.

A woman described how she had scolded God for not stepping up to his responsibility in a difficult situation. Feeling she had done everything she possibly could, she wanted to remind him that there was something there for him to do. God the Father has broad shoulders. He will listen to our complaints as well as to our words of adoration. What he wants is our ongoing dialogue and our movement toward wholeness.

For an easy introduction to reading the words of God, explore the Psalms. In these beautiful and poetic prayers, God's people recounted the many times he showered them with goodness and blessings. They also complained or lamented when they felt abandoned. Sometimes God was chided for his apparent forgetfulness or lack of caring. The Old Testament people felt comfortable speaking to God. Just reading their complaints helps us to realize that we, too, can speak honestly to the Father from the depths of our hearts.

As you read and pray through the Psalms, you will begin to deepen your relationship with the Father. We have many needs and God knows each of them. God, our Father, wants to heal our sicknesses. He wants to take away our sadness. He knows our needs better than we do and he wants to help us. When we talk to God, he listens. We are children of Abba, another word for Daddy. (Rom 8:15) Daddy wants us to tell him about our brokenness. Abba wants a conversion, a transformation of our hearts.

He wants our abandonment to him. Abba is inviting us to come to him.

God the Father loves us so much he sent his own Son to redeem us through death and suffering on the cross. Jesus, Son of the Father, is the Word spoken by him. He came into the world as a man so that we would know the Father's love.

After gaining familiarity with the Book of Psalms, you can begin to know Jesus through his own teachings and stories in the New Testament. He is the fulfillment of Old Testament prophecies, the Messiah, our Teacher and Saviour. Jesus not only reveals the love of his Father, he also reveals the tender and compassionate mercy of God by healing the afflicted. Through his dual role as God and man, he challenges us to a higher standard for living.

Just as God guided Moses and his people on their long journey to the Promised Land, he longs to guide us today. The cloud of Yahweh hovered over the Israelites' tabernacle and at night, a fire shown from within the cloud. Whenever the cloud arose, they knew it was time to resume their journey. (Ex 40:34–38)

Jesus guaranteed that he would not abandon us. He promised that his Father would send us an Advocate, the Holy Spirit, whom he described as the Spirit of truth. The Holy Spirit comes to us from the Father, through Jesus, to enlighten us with truth, to guide us, and to be our constant intercessor. (Jn 14:17) God keeps his promises. Believe in him. Celebrate his faithfulness and thank him often.

St. Paul explained that the Holy Spirit helps us in our weakness and assists us in our prayer. (Rom 8:26–27) In recognition of our need for the Advocate, Pope Paul VI consecrated the 20th century to the Holy Spirit. When we invite the Holy Spirit into our lives, into our homes, and into our churches, everything changes for the better. The Holy Spirit is the very breath of God, breathed out upon us by the Father, through the Son. It is God's own Spirit who empowers us to live Christ's gospel message.

The sacrament of Confirmation involves an adult commitment to live the faith with the help and guidance of the Holy Spirit. When I was confirmed in the fourth grade, I had only a vague understanding of the Holy Spirit. The true significance of the Spirit and the gifts finally became real to me when I was "born again."

Whatever your experience of the Holy Spirit, there is always more available to you. Many who have received the Holy Spirit are unaware of the gifts they have received. Those whose faith is renewed through the Holy Spirit experience a reawakening to the presence of God in their lives.

At a retreat, Episcopalian theologian Morton Kelsey explained the difference between being once-born and born again. Those who are once-born have lived their faith fully from the very beginning. They have always known a special relationship with God. Some of us need a second experience (Baptism in the Spirit) before our faith comes fully alive.

It is through the empowerment of the Holy Spirit that we are able to respond to God's love and to do great things in his name. When you are open to the guidance of the Spirit, your life is transformed and you eagerly step out in faith to live the gospel message.

Opening to the Holy Spirit is not as difficult as it may seem. First, you need to become comfortable with yourself. God loves you unconditionally. He loves you just the way you are right now, with your failings and weaknesses, with your sins and complaints. His unconditional love means that he accepts you now, but he calls you to become all that you can be. As you learn to accept yourself, God's transforming work in you begins and you more fully appreciate the wonderful creation you are.

†††

LOVE, RECONCILIATION, AND PEACE

When you are not in right relationship with God, you suffer. It is impossible to feel peace when you are angry or separated from God.

Because he loves you unconditionally, God accepts you just as you are today. He loves you in spite of your bad habits, your sinful ways, and your lack of attention to him. He waits patiently for you to look his way. When you are open and mindful of his presence, he will bless every aspect of your life.

Abba, God our Daddy, wants you to climb up on his lap and be comfortable. He wants you to trust your loving Father who wants only what is best for his children. He wants to remove any barriers that separate you from his love.

Read Psalm 145. Reflect on the goodness of the Lord who is kind, merciful, slow to anger, compassionate, faithful, holy, just in all his ways, and near to all who call upon him in truth. Is this the Lord you know?

Read Psalm 38. At some time in your life, you may have felt deep guilt over an act or omission. Can you identify with the feeling of separation from God's love that attends sinfulness? Has your heart throbbed with self-accusation and have your eyes lost the light of peace and happiness? Others have felt the same and the Father understands.

Read Psalm 44. Have you known hurt and frustration over some need which you feel God has ignored? Have you felt abandoned daily? Is your patience running out? Do you want to say, "Wake up, Lord! Why are you asleep?"

Write your own psalm. Feel free to praise and thank God for his many blessings, or to complain to him about the times you felt deserted. Describe your pain. Express repentance for the times you turned away from his unconditional love. Close with praise and thanksgiving, and your firm promise to improve your life.

25

As your trust in Abba grows, you will feel comfortable putting your hand in the hand of his Son and walking with him. Jesus longs to teach you the way of Love. When you are ready, he will invite you to be his disciple.

Close your eyes and meditate on the name *Jesus*. What pictures come into your mind? Read the following scriptures slowly and thoughtfully. Spend time prayerfully reflecting upon them: John 6:28–71; John 8:25–30; Romans 8:28–30.

Close your eyes and see the face of Jesus. Look deep into his eyes. Do you see his gentleness? His compassion? His unconditional love? His suffering? Can you see his face in others? Can you be his face to others?

Read Mark 8:27–29. Who is Jesus to you? How do you know him? Where are you looking for him? Are you finding him? Become comfortable with Jesus as your confidante.

Because we need a lot of help in life, Jesus sent us his own Spirit to enlighten and guide us. The Holy Spirit helps us to pray and bestows special gifts which empower us to work for Jesus.

Meditation:
Imagine yourself at a special party. People shower you with affection. They affirm you. They appreciate you. You feel so loved. It is time to open your presents and you are surprised to see gift boxes which have been on your closet shelf for a long time. They have never been opened. The ribbons and wrappings are still in place. Perhaps you were afraid to open them, or you may have thought they belonged to someone else. You are amazed and thrilled at the newness of the gifts which have waited so long for you to discover them. You finally feel ready to use these gifts. The Holy Spirit, the Giver of gifts, will teach you how to use them.

3. Wonderful You

"And if we are children we are heirs as well:
heirs of God and coheirs with Christ...."
(Rom 8:17)

You are so special! You are sons and daughters of a loving King who called you into being, fashioned you in your mother's womb, and named you even before you were born. He invites you to claim your inheritance.

You are heirs through the love of the Father, and you are assured of your inheritance through the redemptive act of his own Son. Even though we were born into sin, we had value, we were worth saving. Christ's complete and loving sacrifice paid the price for our sins, thereby restoring our rights as heirs to the kingdom.

If we are such special children of the King, why do we sometimes feel worthless, abandoned, unloved, and unlovable? How can favored heirs to the kingdom of God suffer from such low self-esteem? We all struggle with such feelings at one time or another. The roots of these feelings could lie in the past and they may even be hidden from your conscious mind.

You were known and loved by God even before conception. When your parents participated with the Creator in the formation of your new life, a single cell began to multiply and grow. That tiny fertilized egg from which you developed contained all of the genetic information necessary to make you the unique and wonderful baby you were becoming.

Newborn babies appear so pure and innocent, seemingly as unsullied as newfallen snow. Yet even before birth, they may have experienced emotions for which they have no words. If they could speak, they might tell us about their ordeals in the womb. By the time you developed the language to explain your feelings, those early memories were deeply buried in your unconscious mind.

Your life began at the moment of conception. By the time your mother knew she was pregnant, you had already achieved amazing development. Your brain developed during the first two months in the womb. While we do not know exactly when or how memory develops, babies often recognize the voices or the music they heard before birth.

Each of us arrives with our quickly forgotten prenatal baggage and a unique personal story begins to develop. Even though you are a beloved child of God, you are also the child of imperfect human parents who bear their own emotional scars. Very real problems sometimes spoil the joy parents would otherwise feel about their little blessed event. That wonderful treasure so desired by the King—that bundle of joy named You—may have shown up at a difficult time in your parents' lives.

Many factors had a bearing on your early life. Were you the first born child? The middle child? The baby? What were your family's financial circumstances before and after you arrived? Were your parents in good health? Did they have a happy marriage? Or any marriage at all?

Not only are we born into varied cultures and different economic circumstances, each of us experiences life from a unique perspective. It is probable that personality is at least partially determined in the womb. Look into any nursery of newborns and observe the quiet, stoic babies alongside of the screamers. Where did they learn their behavior?

A child's personality continues to be shaped by the love that is received, by the way that love is perceived, and by the way that child learns to value himself. Even in the most balanced, loving home, two children raised at the same time by the same parents will have different experiences of love.

Just as we experience parental love differently, we also have different personal experiences of the Father's love. Yet there is one common thread in every life: God called you by name, you are his. (Is 49:1) Our loving Father knows all about our different experiences of love and acceptance. He understands the problems we endure and the struggles life presents to each of us. He also knows the royal person that you can become. You are precious in his sight, a diamond in the rough who is meant to become a gem in his crown.

If you think of a diamond as a brilliant stone, you are correctly describing the finished product. A diamond fresh from the mines may have raw beauty, but is only after cutting, grinding, and polishing that a lustrous gem with refractive properties is revealed. Then, light shone on the perfected stone is reflected in a dispersion of dazzling colors.

JESUS HEALS THE PAST AS WELL AS THE PRESENT

To insure that we become the gems we are intended to be, the Father gave us his Son to heal our hurts and brokenness. The life difficulties you have experienced are part of the cutting and grinding process that shaped you. Jesus provides the final polishing to bring out the true luster hidden within. He releases the fire and light which identify you as an heir of his Father, made in his own image.

No matter what hurts you have received in life, the power of Jesus can heal them. There is nothing too difficult for him. What matters most is that God did not abandon you after he created you. He has always been right there with you, even though you may not have been aware of his presence. He wants to heal you and make you whole, and he will if you allow him.

In a poem that described his impoverished human spirit and also recognized his oneness with Christ, Gerard Manley Hopkins called himself both potsherd and immortal diamond.[4] How can this paradox be explained? We are humans filled with imperfections and riddled with sins. However, through Christ's redemptive act we are invited to outgrow our human frailties and be transformed into gemstones. When Christ dwells within us, we become images of the living God.

In human weakness, we find it easier to flee from our problems than to probe the wounds within. At one point, after months of therapy, I was exhausted from struggling with my problems. I longed to escape for a while. A retreat led by Jean

Vanier[5] sounded like just the tonic I needed. I looked forward to a quiet week in San Diego, enjoying the sun and the beach. This promised to be a time of rest and prayer, an opportunity to recharge my spiritual batteries.

THE HUMAN DESIRE TO AVOID PAIN

Had I anticipated an encounter with my own brokenness, I might have stayed home and missed a deep healing experience. *Blessed Are You*[6] was a retreat for the Faith and Sharing Communities that minister to people with mental or physical disabilities. Jean Vanier is known for the establishment of L'Arche, numerous communities throughout the world where loving care is provided for people with special needs. This retreat was unlike any I had ever experienced. I had never had much contact with developmentally disadvantaged people.

I was immediately drawn in by the simplicity, the joy, the happy songs, and the love of these little ones. They seemed uncomplicated, at least on the surface, and I envied them. Naively, I thought perhaps I could learn from them how to simplify my own life. If I could combine their gift of simplicity with my own gift of intelligence, I would become a better, more spiritual person. It sounded so easy!

From the beginning, we were challenged to listen to the call of Jesus in our hearts, and I made a commitment to do just that. What an ideal setting, I thought, for getting in touch with my inner child. I hoped that I could also learn to have more patience with people in my own life. What I didn't realize was how much healing was needed by that little kid within me!

Vanier's face radiated love and peace as he delivered the message of Christ's Beatitudes. He said, "If God loves me as I am today with all my brokenness, I can accept myself, I can love myself. I don't have to stay caught in a cycle of anger and depression. I can love myself and love my body." Vanier had the countenance of a saint and his words were like honey. I hurriedly took notes and wanted to believe him.

WE NEED EACH OTHER

One evening, we had a candlelight procession. Everyone left the auditorium and walked along a road in darkness to a bluff overlooking the distant lights of the city. Each one carried a candle. It was not an easy journey. The path was uneven. Some were stumbling. Some were in wheelchairs and on crutches. Others limped along. Some were blind. We helped each other. Those of us who were physically able learned to walk slowly because those ahead of us could not hurry.

At times we walked in total darkness. As the wind swirled around us and quenched our tiny flames, we had to relight each other's candles. Some young people needed comfort and reassurance in the dark, while others laughed with glee. There were many lessons to be learned on that journey.

Finally, at the bluff, John's gospel was read: "...Light came into the world and the darkness knew it not..." The gospel came alive. This profound journey spoke volumes about how little and helpless each one of us is in the dark. We learned how badly we all need each other.

The retreat was filled with dramatic lessons. Some were immediate and some required processing. We were on a journey of healing and each person would experience healing where it was most needed.

A story told by Father Jim O'Donnell[7] early in the retreat prepared the way for healing of my self-image. A priest received an exquisite Waterford crystal chalice from his parishioners. As he carried the lovely chalice to the rectory, it slipped from his hands and broke into myriad pieces at his feet. The priest marveled at the shattered glass on the sidewalk, saying, "How beautiful!" There was beauty in the brokenness of the chalice because it reflected even more light than before.

The story of the crystal chalice was thought-provoking, but I did not yet understand how it applied to my life. When I looked around me, I could not overlook the physical or mental disabilities of many retreatants. Some had both. I had neither, but there are other kinds of disabilities besides the obvious impairments. For some of us, the limitations are hidden deep inside, out of public view. They are, however, no less painful.

I reflected on the image of broken crystal and began to wonder if there could be any beauty hidden within my own brokenness. At that point, it was still a matter of idle curiosity.

LISTENING WITH THE HEART

As the retreat progressed, we were drawn deeper and deeper into our own wounds. It was a painful experience for me and not at all what I had expected. I was anticipating rest and refreshment, but now I felt more emotionally drained than when I had first arrived. I even considered leaving the retreat, but I finally decided to see it through. I had promised myself I would listen for the call of Jesus in my heart, so I waited. Then I heard the deeply moving testimony of a young man.

John Winters' physical impairment confined him to a wheelchair and he spoke with great difficulty. Yet his message touched the hearts of everyone who heard him. At one time he had hated himself, hated his body. He felt it was so unfair! He had a good mind but he was angry with God about his body. Then, at catechism class, a Sister taught him each day to love one thing about himself.

Now he could honestly say, "I love my body!" He said, "I am the temple of the Holy Ghost. I give glory to God with my body. People see God in me." When he speaks to groups of school children, they ask, "If you could have one wish, would you want a different body?" His answer is, "No way! I love myself just the way I am."[8]

John's testimony brought tears to my heart as well as to my eyes. He had found the strength to overcome the terrible anger he once felt about his disabling physical condition. His message gave me hope. That evening, I shared with John about my own feelings of inferiority and self-loathing. Perhaps I could learn to love myself too! He pulled me closer so I could hear him and said, "You can do it! Just love yourself a little more each day!"

The eloquent words of Jean Vanier carried the same message as John's halting but powerful speech. He talked about the wounds of childhood and helped us to see their positive value. Those wounds may include the guilt we carry, our broken sexuality, our poor self-image, all the dark things that torment us. We tend to keep these things hidden deep within because we find it so painful to look at them.

Vanier says that Jesus puts his finger on our point of brokenness and says, "I am hidden there." We must open up the pit of darkness and let the light come in. It is there that Jesus wants to meet us. He encourages us to hear the plea of Jesus, "Give me all that is broken inside of you, and it is there you will become a source of life."

This was the call of Jesus in my heart. My head had always known that I should learn to accept and love myself. The difference was that now I knew it in my heart. I knew it in the depths of my brokenness. Jesus found me so lovable he was hidden in the very place within that I had wanted to avoid.

The process of healing my self-image began at that retreat. Some months later, at a Day of Renewal with the theme "Road to Emmaus," I knelt in prayer before the Eucharist and received the following interior message:

"My children, I have invited you into relationship from the very beginning. Open your hearts to me—turn your faces to the light. Let the light of Jesus shine through you so that others will be drawn. Just as the men walking away from Jerusalem, on the road to Emmaus, walked away from the source of light (Jesus) and felt despondent—many of my children are in darkness. Be that tiny spark of light through which others will be warmed and turned toward me."

This message was followed by the mental image of glass shattered into many pieces and reflecting brilliant light. I thanked Jesus for the healing he was accomplishing in me. As I remembered the promise of Jesus, delivered by Jean Vanier, I knew that Jesus would make good use of my brokenness:

> "Give me all that is broken inside of you, and it is there you will become a source of life."[9]

Like those in the candlelight procession, we walk in darkness and the journey is difficult. We try not to look at the brokenness within. It hurts too much. There is beauty in our brokenness but we need someone to help us see it.

AN INVITATION FROM JESUS

Jesus wants to walk with you. His light makes a difference. When you embrace your pain and walk in his light, you begin to see the hidden beauty. You are different from splintered fragments of crystal that briefly shine in the sun before they are swept up and discarded. Jesus is hidden in your brokenness, waiting for you to meet him there.

You are a gemstone in the making, born into royalty, even though at times you feel shattered. Your Father loves you unconditionally and waits patiently for you to come into your full inheritance. Before Jesus departed this earth, he reassured us that he was returning to the Father to prepare a place for us. Then he will return to take us there. Jesus said:

> I am the Way, the Truth and the Life. No one can come to the Father except through me. If you know me, you know my Father too. (Jn 14:6–7)

Christ is the image of the Father. (Col 1:15) When you look upon the face of Jesus, allowing his light and glory to fill your countenance, your face becomes the mirrored reflection of the brightness of the Lord. (2 Cor 3:18) Through his light and glory, you grow brighter and brighter as you are transformed into the image that you reflect. In deep communion with Jesus, your mind will be at peace and your heart will burst forth with song.

✝ ✝ ✝

HIDDEN TREASURE

Can you begin to accept yourself as you are and simply thank God for the brokenness of your life? There is beauty waiting to be discovered in the dark and hidden recesses within you, buried beneath the shame and guilt. Jesus wants to meet you there. He wants to heal you so that his light can shine within you. Are you willing to lovingly explore the anguish that you try so hard to ignore? You really can begin to love yourself. Let him help you.

Write a brief story of your life, beginning with your earliest memories and noting the highlights. Include any significant events, whether good or bad. Now look for the times that God's presence was felt by you and for the times you felt abandoned. (Even though God is always present to us, we are not always present to him.)

Label two columns: "Blessed" and "Abandoned." In the appropriate column, list your significant life events and set aside time every day to pray about them. Thank God for the times you have felt his love. Ask him to heal the anguish of those dark times when you were not aware of his nearness. Thank him for being there even when you could not find him.

A gift is an expression of love and God's precious gift of life to you is an incredible expression of his love. You may have heard it said that the gift without the giver is empty. Could God give you a gift that did not contain his love, that did not embody himself? When you devalue yourself, you devalue the giver of the gift.

What I am is God's gift to me. What I become is my gift to God![10]

Embrace yourself, with all of your flaws and mistakes. Cherish the gift that you are. Acceptance is the first step toward becoming all that God wants you to be. Perhaps you see only your imperfections and miss the inner beauty that God sees in you. He doesn't reject your brokenness. He sees your great potential and loves the whole person. When you accept and embrace your true self, you embrace God himself. As you do so, your heart overflows with praise for him.

Meditate on Psalm 139:13–15:

> It was you who created my inmost self,
> and put me together in my mother's womb;…
> You know me through and through,
> from having watched my bones take shape
> when I was being formed in secret
> knitted together in the limbo of the womb.

4. The Language of Love

"Prayer is the song of the heart."[11]

Now that you are better able to see yourself as the Father sees you, your heart can sing a new song to the Lord! (Is 42:10) Jesus is teaching you to love and accept yourself as he loves and accepts you. He now invites you to continue the journey with him as your guide.

There is more to prayer than reciting words. Prayer is our intimate dialogue with God. If you are invited to an audience with royalty, you wear your best clothing and polish your manners, hoping to make a good impression. Jesus calls you to an audience with the Holy of Holies. You must enter with a clean heart and a pure mind when you speak to God.

> I tell you therefore: everything you ask and pray for, believe that you have it already, and it will be yours. And when you stand in prayer, forgive whatever you have against anybody, so that your Father in heaven may forgive your failings too. (Mk 11:24–25)

Wow! Anything I ask and pray for? Just believe that I have it and it will be mine? But wait! What about the last part? Not that! Do I have to forgive *everyone?*

The expectations of Jesus are great, but he promises treasure to those who follow in his footsteps. Jesus extends his hands to you. In one, he offers you the power of prayer. Whatever you ask in faith will be granted. His other hand is outstretched to you, waiting for you to forgive as his Father forgives. It would be inappropriate to expect to receive power from the one hand, without placing your forgiveness in the other.

Jesus understands what he is asking. Remember, he knows your every thought, your failings, and your weaknesses. Is there someone you need to forgive? Let him help you. Begin by making a sincere act of your will to forgive. No matter how atrocious the offense of another, you can forgive them through the love of Jesus. Even as he hung bleeding and dying on the cross, Jesus forgave the repentant criminal who hung next to him, assuring him a place in heaven.

Once you have made the intention to forgive the one who has wronged you, continue to pray for the grace to repair your broken relationship. Don't be concerned if you don't feel any different. Your choice to forgive is a decision based on reason. Feelings are simply feelings and cannot be controlled. You can, however, control how you act on them.

Avoid nurturing any feelings of resentment, anger, or hurt. Hand them to Jesus and ask him to accept your sincere decision to forgive. In time, he will replace those feelings with his love. When you experience the release of all that negativity, you will know the true joy of a forgiving heart.

When Jesus taught us how to pray the Lord's Prayer, he made it clear that we must also seek forgiveness from anyone whom we have harmed. That can be more difficult than forgiving because pride enters in. Will you look foolish? What if that person refuses to accept your apology? Perhaps they will hang up on your call or turn and walk away from you. What if you are unable to find that person and make amends?

Again, it is the intention of your heart that matters most. When your desire is sincere and you do all that you can to correct your transgressions against another, God's grace will supply all that you need to accomplish this. (2 Cor:12–9)

When we are freed from the sinfulness of our broken relationships, our prayers ascend to the Father with a beautiful fragrance. Once our lives are in the right order and we are in harmony with God, we begin to see his power at work in answer to our prayers.

The health of your relationships reflects your relationship with God, just as it reveals how much you truly love yourself. You cannot feel comfortable in God's presence if you are at war with yourself, your friends, your relatives, or others. Even after you have repaired old relationships, there is no guarantee that you won't have such problems in the future. The difference is that you will be prepared to mend them quickly.

> You must therefore be perfect just as your heavenly Father is perfect. (Mt 5:48)

HOW CAN I BE PERFECT?

What God desires from us is not the perfection*ism* we sometimes demand of ourselves. Perfection is not so much a destination as it is journey, since only God is perfect. What he wants is our continual striving towards perfect love. He loves us in spite of all the ways that we are not perfect, and this is the kind of love he desires us to give to others. His call to perfection is summed up in two rules that Jesus gave us. When a Pharisee asked which was the greatest commandment of the Law, Jesus answered:

> You must love the Lord your God with all your heart, with all your soul, and with all your mind. This is the greatest and the first commandment. The second resembles it: You must love your neighbor as yourself. (Mt 22:37–39)

It is a contradiction to say "I love God but I hate myself!" Likewise, if you can't tolerate yourself, how can you fulfill the second commandment to love your neighbor? As you nurture your relationship with God by deepening your prayer life, all of your relationships will be altered.

The story is told that a traveler who stooped to pick up a shrivelled leaf was surprised by the lovely perfume of the dry leaf. "Oh, you poor withered leaf," he exclaimed, "whence comes this exquisite perfume?" The leaf replied, "I have lain for a long time in the company of a rose."[12]

When you are immersed in a loving relationship with God, strengthened by a loving acceptance of yourself as his special creation, your entire being is transformed. People see the love of God shining through you and you begin to recognize God in the faces of others. Like the leaf, you emanate the characteristics of the One to whom you are close.

PRAYER RESHAPES YOUR HEART

Prayer is the means by which you attain this newness. Prayer, communication with God, is the key element in your relationship with him. Your ongoing prayer reshapes your heart into a welcoming receptacle for Jesus. In a famous picture, Jesus stands in front of a closed door, waiting. Since there is neither latch nor handle on the outside, the door can only be opened from within. Jesus will be present in your life only if you welcome him. Opening your heart through prayer makes it possible for Jesus to enter.

When you truly love someone, you long to be with them. You cherish opportunities to spend time together. You want to know all about that person and you want to share yourself fully. The same is true of your love relationship with Jesus, who stands ready to lead you to the Father.

Jesus wants to spend time with you. He waits. Sometimes he waits for days, hoping you will become aware of his presence. The world is a busy place, so full of distractions. We are easily deterred from spending time in prayer. These impediments, however, can only interfere with our prayer when we allow them to. By placing a value on your prayer life, you make a commitment to improving it. Set aside time, no matter how busy your schedule, to be in God's presence.

One early autumn day, I watched workers preparing the strawberry fields for planting. While it seemed a bit early to be thinking about summer fruit, the sight of the laborers reminded me that tomorrow's ripe red berry has its start in today's planting. If you begin the work of tilling your prayer garden today, you can also begin to anticipate the rewards of tomorrow's rich harvest, rewards that are greater than you can imagine.

> ...where a man sows, there he reaps...
> if he sows in the field of the Spirit
> he will get from it a harvest of eternal life.
> (Gal 6:7–8)

Another time, I returned from a trip to discover that the leaves of my little prayer plant had turned brown and crisp. I revived the dying plant with water and in a very short time, new leaves began to sprout. From its perch on the windowsill, it greeted each day by stretching and opening to the warmth of the sun. At night, it solemnly folded its leaves in prayer. This plant reminded me to nurture my prayer life by opening my heart to the warmth of the Son each morning, and by thanking God for his blessings at the end of every day.

It helps to question yourself from time to time. Has your prayer life become dry and brittle? Is it dying in small degrees because you have forgotten to nurture it? Prayer needs to be renewed and cultivated. Reciting the prayers you have committed to memory is good but your spiritual life can grow far beyond that point. As you put new life into your prayer, ask God to breathe vitality into your relationship with him.

REINVENT YOUR PRAYER LIFE

Your union with God will be enriched as you discover new and better ways to speak to him. Dialogue is two-way communication. As you bring a freshness to your relationship, you can also learn to listen for God's whisperings to you. This conversation, which can have a variety of expressions, need never be boring or routine. There are many ways to pray.

Prayers of adoration flow out of our recognition that God is God. They also acknowledge our own lowliness as mere creatures in his holy presence. Through adoration, we humbly accept our Creator as the all-powerful, all-knowing, all-just, and all-loving God that he is. Our praise and adoration also profess our rightful relationship with him.

Our hearts are lifted on wings of prayer when we read and repeat prayers of praise, such as those found in the Psalms. Prayers of adoration and praise are pleasing to God, so much so that he created angels whose job is to praise him constantly. It has been said that he who sings, prays twice and St. Paul encourages believers to constantly sing and give thanks to God. (Eph 5:19–20)

Once on a retreat, I sought counseling about a troubled family member. While I was powerless to act in the situation, I felt compelled to do something. I was advised to simply kneel for one hour in adoration of the Holy Eucharist. During that hour I had a profound prayer experience. By totally surrendering the problem to Jesus, I was admitting that even though I am powerless, he is all-powerful. Not only was I comforted, the situation improved without my interference. My trust in Jesus was rewarded.

The celebration of the Eucharist, which Jesus instituted at the Last Supper, incorporates many forms of prayer: adoration, praise, reconciliation, thanksgiving, petition, and intercession. By receiving Communion, one *comes into union* with Jesus as the vessel for his holy presence.

The more time you spend in God's presence, the more you hunger for deeper intimacy with him. The prayer of meditation requires self-discipline but it brings rich rewards. First and foremost, you need to set aside a quiet time and a place to meditate. You may need to close your bedroom door and post a "Do Not Disturb" sign in order to insure uninterrupted prayer time.

Begin by assuming a comfortable position. Some people prefer to lie down while others are more comfortable sitting. If you sit, choose a chair that will keep your back straight. With your feet firmly on the ground, your hands resting in your lap, and your eyes closed, you are prepared for an encounter with God.

There will be distractions at first. Your nose may itch or your feet may want to move. Your mind will wander in every direction imaginable. It helps to focus on the breath that goes in and out of your nose. As you breathe in deeply, let your mind say, "Jesus," and with the slow exhalation of breath, "loves me." Repeat this again and again, allowing the muscles in your feet, your legs and on upward throughout your body to go limp. Inhale "Jesus"…exhale "loves me."

Unlike some forms of meditation that aim to empty the mind, Christian meditation centers on Jesus. As you eliminate distractions, you focus instead on his overpowering love. Let Jesus lead you in the meditation.

Pictures may emerge in your mind, or perhaps there will be

colors or words. Accept these gifts and allow Jesus to speak his word within you. Avoid letting the little graces of image or words become more important than your concentration on Jesus. If no images come, simply rest in the silence of his presence, with full knowledge that Jesus knows what is best for you at this time. Allow him to touch your soul. There is power in the prayer of meditation.

If sounds distract you, center your mind once again on your breathing, repeating "Jesus—loves me." When you are ready to end the meditation, slowly open your eyes and gently awaken your body. Do not jump up quickly, but rather leave the meditative state as carefully as you entered it. You will be refreshed and filled with an inner peace. Thank the Lord for sharing this special time with you. Make an appointment to meet with him on a regular basis.

Initially, your meditation may last only a few minutes. Be patient with yourself. After a while, your meditation may last for twenty or thirty minutes. For variety, you may find it useful to use phrases of scripture or to imagine yourself in a Biblical setting with Jesus as he teaches and heals. Discover the many areas in which he wants to heal you.

RESTING IN HIS PRESENCE

In contemplative prayer, you share your heart with Jesus. There is nothing that you need to say because he already knows the depths of your heart. During this special state of prayer, which can flow out of the practice of meditation, your heart will long for Jesus just as the Bride longs for the Bridegroom in the Song of Solomon. In contemplation, you simply rest in the presence of Jesus, asking nothing, wanting only to be in his holy place.

The great mystic Saint Teresa of Avila likened contemplative prayer to the warm sharing that occurs between close friends. It is a sacred time of friendship and love, a time without interruptions. Heart to heart and face to face with God, you begin to hear his whispers.

Our prayer life should include adoration and worship of God, repentance for the times we failed to love, and thanksgiving

for his many blessings. We come on bended knee before our
Maker and honor his sovereignty over our lives. We also have
many needs and concerns and we are encouraged by Christ to
bring our worries to him:

> Whatever you ask for in my name I will do, so that the
> Father may be glorified in the Son. If you ask for anything in
> my name I will do it. (Jn 14:13–14)

Our prayers of petition will understandably include our
immediate needs and those of our families and friends, but
they should not end there. We have a responsibility to pray
for our neighbors, for the sick and the poor, for the deceased,
for our communities, the world at large, and yes, even for
our enemies. At the center of our prayer should be a joining
of our hearts with the heart of Christ, who loves saints and
sinners alike and who prays for the coming of his Father's
kingdom.

God wants our minds and hearts focused on him and while
that is the primary purpose of our prayer, it is important to realize that we need prayer more than he does. Prayers keep our
minds centered on him but they also comfort us. St. Paul's pre-
scription for prayer is not easy. He challenges us to be happy at
all times, to pray constantly, and to give thanks to God for all
things. (1 Thes 5:17–18) Can we, indeed, pray constantly when
there are so many duties that demand our attention? How can
we thank God for the bad things that happen? And how is it possible for anyone to be happy all of the time?

It was during a seminar on spirituality that I learned to
pray constantly. Any wholesome act can become a prayer
when that is your intention. Whether it is dinner with
friends, a quiet moment spent listening to fine music, or an
unpleasant chore, your conscious intention can transform
these moments into prayer. Even your service to others can
be prayers of humility. With your mind set on God, your
entire life becomes prayer. While we still need other forms of
prayer, we can elevate the most common activities to the
realm of spiritual communication. Yes, it is possible to pray
constantly.

DANCING ON HOT COALS

Giving thanks for all things is a pretty large order. Merlin Carothers describes being rescued from a life of crime and dishonor when he chose Jesus to be his Savior. His book *Prison to Praise*[13] is filled with stories about God's generosity when Carothers praised and thanked the Lord for troubled situations.

Catherine Marshall elaborates on this theme in *Something More*.[14] She describes her struggle to accept tragic circumstances in her own life. She also recounts Corrie Ten Boom's experiences in a Nazi concentration camp as further proof that God can bring good out of any circumstances. She defines praise as the "golden bridge to the heart of God," because we look away from our problems when we look with trust and confidence at Jesus.

Praise is powerful. The three young men in the fiery furnace walked in the heart of the flames, blessing the Lord. As they raised their voices in song, exalting the wonders of God and celebrating his praise in all of nature, an angel of the Lord was with them. When Nebuchadnezzar's eyes were opened to the power and glory of the Lord, he ordered the men released from the furnace. They were miraculously unharmed. (Dn 3)

Dancing on hot coals is not easy, nor is this an easy way to pray. Giving thanks and praise when things go wrong does not come naturally. Human nature wants to struggle against God's plan. We think we need to tell God how to answer our prayers. In my own life, I have learned that when I relinquish my burdens and give them totally to Jesus with praise and thanksgiving, amazing things happen. When we can yield and put all of our trust in him, our prayers are answered in much better ways than we expected.

When you live your life in deep communion with God, you enjoy deep peace and happiness in spite of the travails of the world. This is the happiness Paul described. In the humble posture of adoration, you no longer try to shape God into your image but rather you allow him to be God.

As you continue to experience a deep healing of your prayer life, you find that you are better able to love and accept even those difficult people in your life. By opening to them in love, you begin to notice an even deeper intimacy with God, who makes all things possible.

Unconditional love, the kind of love the Father has for each of us, is a gift which grows in you through your relationship with God. Once you have lain in the company of a rose, you will not settle for less. You will become for others the rose in whose presence they wish to abide.

† † †

THE SONG IN YOUR HEART

In today's busy world, it is difficult to find moments of quiet and repose. With all of the distractions that surround you, you may find it difficult to pray. God wants to refreshen you and bring joy into your prayer life. He is ready to do this if you are willing.

Picture yourself looking out through the window of your house at your prayer garden. Are there weeds growing there? How can you cultivate your garden? Is Jesus outside, knocking at your door? Does he wait for you to welcome him inside? What prevents you from opening the door?

Make a list of the obstacles that discourage you and prevent you from deepening your relationship with God. Discouragement is one of the wearing-out tactics of Satan. By constantly showing you your failings, he convinces you that you are worthless and unlovable. Your salvation through the death of Jesus demonstrates God's unconditional love for you. It is the answer to discouragement. Pray over your list. Ask Jesus to help you release your obsessions. Trust in his providence and abandon your anxieties to his loving care.

Ask God's forgiveness for the times you have allowed yourself to be separated from his love. Forgive yourself and make a resolution to amend your ways.

Meditation:
See Jesus hanging on the cross, his body twisted with pain. His heart overflows with love and compassion for you. Look into his eyes as you place your sins and weaknesses deep into his heart. Tell him how sorry you are for causing his suffering. Ask him to help you live a pure and godly life. Now accept his forgiveness. Receive the waters of grace that flow down from the cross, cleansing and refreshing you. Know that you are a lovable child of God.

All creation praises God. Learn from the simplest creatures how to praise God with your life. God is worthy to be praised and you were created to praise and honor him.

Read Psalm 148. Where, today, did you see nature praising God? Perhaps it was in a beautiful sunset, in the song of a bird, in a tiny ant laboring under a heavy load, or in the lacelike web of a spider. Try to become aware of God's intricate and wonderful creations all around you.

Do you suppose God grows tired of hearing his children mindlessly reciting the same words repeatedly while their thoughts wander? Learn to be creative with your prayer. Put your whole being, mind, body and spirit into your communication with God.

Read Psalm 150. Explore ways that you can praise God through music. Do you play a musical instrument? Can you praise him with your talent? Try singing along with a musical praise tape as you drive in your automobile. Your song will be pleasing to God and your journey will be less stressful. Have you ever observed how freely children dance when they are happy? Try praising God in a joyful private prayer by dancing to spiritual music.

Remember how you loved to share secrets as a child? Perhaps there is something special you would like to share with God. Even though he knows your every thought, he loves to hear from you. Share a secret with God.

In Jerusalem, little notes are tucked into the crevices between the stones of the ancient Wailing Wall. The notes are left by visitors of all faiths, who long to send a personal message to God. Recently, a fax line was made available, so that people all over the world can send a message to Yahweh.[15] Write the message you would like to send to God. Sit in quiet prayer and read your message to him. He already knows your heart, but he likes to keep the communication lines open.

5. Jesus Laughed!

"...your hearts will be full of joy...."
(Jn 16:22)

*W*ho is this God-man we call Jesus? *The Catechism of the Catholic Church* explains that Jesus was both God and man. He possessed two natures, one divine and one human, which were "united in the one person of God's Son."

We know that in his human qualities, Jesus must have been a lot like us. Little is written about his early childhood but it is safe to assume that it was relatively normal. In his three years of public ministry, Jesus displayed a wide range of emotions. He loved, he wept, he grieved, and he suffered. He showed righteous anger in the temple.

Because his ministry was demanding and tiring, Jesus and his disciples sometimes hid from the crowds that gathered wherever he went. Yet whenever the people sought him out and found him, he always responded with compassionate healing of the sick and tender mercy for sinners. Jesus did more than talk about compassion and mercy, he showed us so that we could learn and remember.

When the hour of his crucifixion approached, Jesus knelt and pleaded with his Father for mercy but he concluded obediently, "Nevertheless, let your will be done, not mine." (Lk 22:42) A man of deep emotions, Jesus did not consider it unmanly to acknowledge feelings of fatigue and sadness. It was through the empowerment of his divine nature, the grace of the Holy Spirit within, that he was able to rise above those human feelings to show extraordinary compassion and love toward those who came to him.

Nowhere in Scripture are we told that Jesus laughed. His first public miracle occurred at a festive wedding. A typical wedding

49

feast in his time included a considerable amount of eating and drinking, accompanied by music, dancing and merriment. It may have lasted as long as seven days.[16] Do you think Jesus sat with a long face at the wedding feast? Or did he sing, dance, and laugh with the other guests?

Jesus is frequently portrayed sharing a meal with friends. People were attracted to him. He had charisma. Did Jesus laugh? While there is no written proof that he did, common sense tells us that this well-balanced man was in full control of his emotions and freely expressed his joy with hearty laughter.

WHAT DID JESUS LAUGH ABOUT?

What do you suppose Jesus laughed about? Perhaps he laughed at his distraught parents when they found him in the Temple. He knew that he wasn't lost and he might have eased his parents' tension and defused their anger with his boyish laughter. Perhaps he said, "Mother, I was hoping you would come. I am so hungry!" On hearing that, Mary would have laughed too. She must have had an inkling of the strong man her boy would become.

Of the twelve ordinary men chosen by Jesus to carry on his ministry, at least six were fishermen. They were strong, muscular men capable of hauling in cumbersome fishing nets loaded with the daily catch. Two were called "Sons of Thunder," perhaps for their hot tempers. The treasurer was a betrayer. One apostle had been a tax collector and another was a skeptic. One may have belonged to the Zealots, who fought the Romans in defense of their belief in the One God. Peter, upon whom Christ would build his church, was rash and impulsive, loyal and loving. What did this unlikely assortment of men have in common?

The Twelve were probably earthy, practical men with a zestful love for life. Simon Peter and Andrew dropped their fishing nets to follow Jesus, literally trading their livelihood for ministry. Men of character, they shared a strong dedication and commitment to Jesus. These common men chosen by Jesus would become fishers of souls for the kingdom.

Imagine Jesus relaxing with his friends after a day of preaching and healing. These were undoubtedly robust, good-humored men with hearty laughs. They must have shared jokes and fellowship, and they surely had many stories to tell. In a spirit of camaraderie, they probably engaged in a lot of teasing and horseplay.

Simon Peter had a gift for acting impulsively and for speaking first and thinking later. Jesus and his companions must have laughed often, in a loving and brotherly way, at blustering Peter's imperfections. Jesus, who loved to tell stories, had so much to teach his followers during his three years of ministry. Like other great teachers, he probably used humor to make his point. Laughter would have brought balance to the seriousness of their mission.

LAUGHTER IS GOOD MEDICINE

Humor is an important teaching tool, and an old adage reminds us that laughter is the best medicine. Just as tears heal by releasing painful emotions, laughter plays an equally important role in emotional health. Norman Cousins proved the healing properties of laughter by using humorous films to aid his recovery from a debilitating illness. He also furthered research and promoted awareness of the healing powers of laughter and a positive attitude.[17]

What are the physical effects of laughter? *Healthy Pleasures*[18] describes laughter as "an affirmation of our humanness." The authors compare the benefits of "inner jogging" (hearty laughter) to a physical workout. They stress that like animals, we have the choice to flee or to fight, but as humans we have another option. We can laugh!

Laughter has a healthy effect on respiration and blood pressure and it relaxes the body and facial muscles. It has been credited with pain relief and the inducement of a long-lasting state of well-being. Also, it may send healthy chemicals to the brain and may help strengthen the immune system. Laughter is a wonderful tool for relieving tension and for diffusing anger. Have you ever tried to sustain your anger while in the throes of a fit of laughter? It cannot be done.

While I was coping with terminal cancer, encircled by a

dynamic husband and six children, there were many occasions for laughter in the midst of tragedy. I had grown up a somber and serious only child. As compensation, God wisely blessed me with a husband whose optimism and laughter transform tears to smiles and giggles. He has a special healing gift.

My husband's hearty and rollicking laugh seems to emanate from deep within him. The sound is a healing balm to my soul. It always brings a smile to my face and warms my heart. Some mornings, I awake to the sound of his vigorous laughter as he reads the morning comics. I can recognize his laughter in a crowd. It is a fingerprint of his personality. His laugh is so generous and real, I have often wished I could package it to share with others who are in need of a lift.

Because I lived in an arena of laughter and good-humor, I learned early to accept a lot of teasing. Up until the time of my cancer, however, my life felt more like a dark travail than a blessing to be enjoyed. All of that changed when God healed my negative attitude.

Early in the course of my cancer, my husband and I watched *Where's Poppa?*, a movie that had me rolling on the floor with laughter. I must admit, I have since watched it without the same hysterical reaction. At the time, however, it was the funniest film I had ever seen. It was a great tonic. I was learning to laugh great belly-laughs and it felt so good!

After the miraculous disappearance of cancer, I followed my doctors' advice and continued the treatments they had planned. Since the cancer had already spread, they fully expected my virulent disease to return. Chemotherapy and radiation treatments, which originally were intended to "buy some time," would provide insurance for the future. Father John McGregor had prudently advised me to be obedient to my doctors. Meanwhile, he prayed that I would not have side effects from the treatments.

LEARN TO LAUGH AT YOURSELF

While I never suffered from nausea and the usual side effects, I was not immune to baldness! This was the era of the great fall-out. My thick, brown, naturally-wavy hair stayed on my pillow when I arose each morning and clumps of it stuck to my hands when I shampooed it. Since I had already purchased a wig, I bravely decided to end the disgusting fall-out and I asked my husband to shave my head.

As I gazed at my bare scalp in the mirror, a pile of shorn hair around my feet, my husband consoled me with the news that my head was beautifully shaped. Because of his affirmation, I knew that he loved me with hair or without. Furthermore, he had already promised that he would paint my head silver and decorate it with stars if I disliked baldness.

While I was adjusting to my changed appearance, there was a tapping on the bathroom door. Patrick, my thirteen-year-old son, wanted to see my new look. My immediate answer was no, but he pleaded, promising not to laugh. Reluctantly, I opened the door and let him in. With a true comic's straight-faced delivery, he said, "Shine your head for a quarter!"

We all had a good laugh—until I tried on my new wig. Without the thick padding of hair, my wig flopped willy-nilly on my head. My laughter quickly turned to tears and I swore I would never be seen in public again! Jesus must have been laughing then, because he knew it was not true. I learned how to alter the wig to fit. Determined to have fun with an undesirable situation, I even obtained several other wigs for different looks. The best part of being bald was mopping my bare head with a cool, wet cloth in the heat of summer.

Actually, by July my new growth of hair was showing promise, but that was short-lived. When a brain scan was ordered to determine the cause of ongoing headaches, the doctor overseeing my radiation treatments reassured me that the scan would have no impact on my new crop. Wrong! The limp fibers stayed on my pillow the next morning. I looked like a billiard ball once again. Jesus was teaching me a lot about laughter! This focus on hair problems helped distract me from my deeper concerns that the cancer might have metastasized. That is a common fear among cancer patients.

Finally, a year after the diagnosis of cancer, I was blessed with a new crop of curly hair. I bravely abandoned wigs and turbans and luxuriated in my short, but real, hair. It was so curly, Afro-style, that I accused the oncologist of dosing me with chemicals that would make my hair look like his. When I later complained that my curls were straightening, he replied, "We don't guarantee curls, Pat. We just guarantee hair!" At last I could join comfortably in the laughter about my hair.

The joy of the Lord surprised me. In the past, I had often felt that nothing was right even when nothing was wrong. With joy came such a good feeling, I immediately recognized it as an important component that had been missing all along. Joy bubbled to the surface and transformed me. A lot of inner healing followed, but the joy came first.

LAUGHTER CAN BE HOLY

During my treatments, a friend and prayer partner sympathized with my emotional roller coaster and sent me a quote from George Macdonald describing "holy laughter."

> "It is the heart that is not yet sure of its God that is afraid to laugh in His presence."[19]

This concept of holy laughter was new to me, but it made sense when I began to understand that Jesus' nature includes a well-developed sense of humor. Since we are made in his image and likeness, this is an aspect of God well worth emulating. I had been trying so hard to live a godly life, but God wanted me to know that laughter is important to our spirituality. He wants us to be whole people. Wholeness means a state of healthy balance. It calls for play as well as work, for laughter as well as for tears.

It is liberating to laugh at ourselves. Once we stop taking ourselves too seriously, the whole world becomes a lighter and lovelier place. Jesus wants to heal us in every way. He wants us to be joyful. He wants us to see the many possibilities for laughter in our lives.

Today, I find it difficult to imagine a God who welcomes somber, lifeless prayers. I believe that the Author of all good things delights in our happiness. Our loving Father blesses our laughter. Not only would Jesus approve of our dancing in church, I believe he would be the first to join us. With Jesus as choreographer, our prayers would be lively expressions of praise, complete with tambourines and drums, trumpets and cymbals, tap shoes and castanets!

Joy may not heal your arthritis but it can make the pain bearable. It may not, by itself, reverse your cancer or mend your damaged nerves and it will not restore lost limbs. However, it might help repair whatever else is wrong in your life. I guarantee that your life will never be the same, once the joy of the Lord makes its home in your heart. His joy will change your attitude and it will alter your response to your circumstances. That one factor alone will cause a dramatic change in your life!

JOY COUNTERBALANCES SORROW

The peace and joy that come from God are not insurance against pain and suffering. Rather, they are the spiritual gifts that will enable you to bear your pain and suffering, by knowing you are securely wrapped in God's love. God will strengthen you today for tomorrow's trials. My story of personal healing would be too much like a fairy tale if I left the impression that the arrival of joy ended all of my suffering. Such was not the case.

When the cancer struck, I had been struggling with some big emotional problems that I believe contributed to my illness. The cancer seemed to be a physical manifestation of old problems that had been literally eating me alive inside.

Through the grace of God and the help of Father McGregor and others, I was able to achieve a lot of inner healing. This was a painful process because I had to probe old wounds in order to open them for healing. In the meantime, life with all of its normal ups and downs continued.

Within days of the onset of my cancer, my daughter had a complete mental breakdown and was given the diagnosis of chronic schizophrenia. Anne, who had seemed to be coping so strongly with my illness, was actually paralyzed with fear over my impending death. Because of the stress she felt, she became lost in an interior world of confusion and isolation. This was a very sad time for our family. Even when my cancer disappeared a month after its diagnosis, the daughter I had known remained lost. God helped us carry that burden.

Meanwhile, God continued to strengthen me so that I would be able to cope with all of the new problems that would arise. After a year of treatments to prevent the cancer's return, my immune system was so weakened I was the target of every virus in town. The most discouraging setback was a severe case of shingles. Unlike ordinary shingles, mine resembled a third degree burn and left me immobilized for weeks. I spent a month in isolation at the hospital, subdued by pain that was unlike any I have ever known. It was then that I asked God, "Why me?" God was silent.

Finally, I submitted totally, saying, "Accept my pain, Lord, as my gift to you…for all who are sick in this hospital with cancer, and for all of the people I have promised my prayers. My pain is all I have to give you now. Use me." While that may sound brave and noble, I felt completely beaten.

Initially, I was frightened and nearly incoherent from huge amounts of pain medication. I felt totally abandoned in the hospital until God gently made his presence known to me. After a distressing night of hallucinations and fear, and a lot of prayer, I awoke to find the hospital chaplain standing at my bedside. When I told him of my fretful night and my desperate prayers, he understood. God, who had been there all the time, had sent this priest to bring me the Eucharist. At last, God's comfort and peace returned.

Later, I realized that God used that experience to strengthen me. He gifted me with a new understanding of pain so that I could empathize with others he would send across my path. Even though my awful ordeal required surgery before my wounded body could heal, I look back on those dark events as a blessing in disguise. The scars that remain are a roadmap of where I have been, a reminder of God's mercy. He gives us all that we need to survive every crisis.

There were other scares in the months and years that followed the cancer experience. A broken rib convinced one doctor that my cancer had returned, even though a bone scan and blood tests were normal. There were X-rays for suspicious lumps that proved to be harmless. Once, I needed a painful and unpleasant bone biopsy to rule out cancer beneath a tooth. The X-ray looked foreboding but things are not always what they seem to be.

God has shown me that I do not walk alone. We cannot walk in fear when we walk with him. When times are tough, I shed a few tears of frustration and then get on with the present moment. Storms pass and sunshine follows. God continues to strengthen me and renew his gift of joy, often showing me the humor hidden within each sorrow.

What prevented me from being a joyful Christian before my cancer experience? I had misunderstood the nature of God. Our personal encounter with the Father can be distorted by the wrong perception that he is a punishing deity. When Isaiah described the messianic era, he listed the prophetic attributes that would distinguish the Messiah from false prophets. The virtues attributed to the Son of God are identical to the Gifts of the Holy Spirit: wisdom, understanding, counsel, fortitude, knowledge, piety, and fear of the Lord. (Is 11:1–3)

Fear is an emotion of dread and fright. How can you love, embrace, trust, and find comfort in a God whom you fear? Reason tells us that the Spirit of God gives us only good gifts that will never separate us from God nor cause our unhappiness.

It was Jesus who revealed to us his gentle Father, who out of boundless love for us, sent his own Son to redeem us. The gift of "fear" means you should have a "reverential wonder and awe of the Lord."[20] You should be moved to admiration, respect, and veneration for his authority and power. Seen in this light, God is approachable and you are drawn to him.

> ...fear is driven out by perfect love:
> because to fear is to expect punishment,
> and anyone who is afraid is still imperfect in love.
> We are to love, then,
> because he loved us first. (1 Jn 4:18–19)

St. Paul said that when the Holy Spirit directs our lives, we will enjoy fruits of the Spirit: love, joy, peace, patience, kindness, goodness, trustfulness (faithfulness), gentleness, and self-control. (Gal 5:22–23)

Serve one another, rather, in works of love, since the whole
of the Law is summarized in a single command: Love your
neighbour as yourself. (Gal 5:13–14)

When we present the face of Christ to the world, people see
his love, joy, and peace radiating from our faces. We become
known for our patience, with ourselves and with others. Our
kindness and goodness show in little ways of thoughtfulness, in
unselfish gestures. Those in pain are drawn by our gentle ways
as we minister God's love to them. Our lives and our actions
become examples to others of faithfulness, self-control, and
integrity.

Living like Christ, being his joyful presence to others, is the
most powerful statement we can make as Christians. Jesus is
calling you to be a disciple. As he continues to touch and heal
you, he invites you to be a joyful sign of his love. He may use
you to bring his healing to those who cross your path. The Jesus
Walk calls for a strong commitment on your part.

† † †

JESUS WANTS YOU TO BE WHOLE AS WELL AS HOLY

Joy implies freedom, a release from tension, and unbounded happiness. Joy is an indication of wholeness and Jesus wants us to be whole as well as holy. A balanced life leads to wholeness. It is easy to become so involved in activities that you lose your perspective. Examine your present life and determine where changes are needed to achieve a proper balance of spirit, mind, and body.

ARE YOU IN OR OUT OF BALANCE?

- Is your life controlled by compulsive behavior? Do you: eat too much? drink too much? talk too much? work too much? sleep too much? worry too much?
- Do you rely on alcohol, drugs, tobacco, or medications to help you cope with nervous tension, restlessness, insomnia, or depression?
- Is there quiet, meditative time in your life?
- Do you manage to get some physical exercise every day?
- Do you make time for playful recreation?
- Do you only associate with people in your own age group?
- Do you eat a well-balanced diet?
- When was your last physical checkup?
- When did you last read a book that stretched your mind?
- Do you take time to get in touch with nature?
- Do you spend all of your time indoors?
- Do you suffer a lot from minor illnesses—colds, flu, rashes, headaches?
- Have you been accident-prone—had a series of falls, collisions, cuts, or other injuries?
- Do you lose your temper over "nothing?" A lot?
- Do you cry too much?
- Do you laugh? Can you laugh when you make a mistake?
- Do you listen to music, enjoy fine art?
- How much time do you spend watching television?
- How much time to you spend in escapist activities?

59

- How much time do you spend in conversation with others?
- Do you have at least one friend in whom you can confide?
- Are you more interested in talking or in listening?
- Are you actively involved in helping others in some way?
- Describe your personal relationship with God.
- How do you measure up against your very best self?
- Are you happy with your answers to these questions? If not, what can you change?

An Ounce of Prevention:

"An apple a day keeps the doctor away." Eat the apple because it is good for you, but thank God daily for the gift of good health. As health care costs soar, more emphasis is being given to the adaptation of a healthy life-style. Wellness involves preventive measures that include proper diet, physical fitness, and emotional stability. A holistic approach includes the spiritual life.

Meditation:

Assume a relaxed position and close your eyes. Imagine a world of darkness. There is only one source of light. You are the lantern through which that light can shine. As the light flows through you, feel the warmth and love radiating outward, dispelling the darkness, and bringing the dawn of new life into the world. Thank Jesus for his light shining through you.

6. Christ at the Center

"Do whatever he tells you." (Jn 2:5)

*W*hen you present Christ's face to the world, the attributes that others see in you flow from his grace. There is no need to worry that you will become puffed-up when you walk with Jesus. On the contrary, you will be humbled. Jesus, whom you seek to imitate, will provide lessons in humility as he walks with you and teaches you. In many ways your journey with Christ will be a path of roses, but even the loveliest roses have thorns.

Jesus warned that his disciples would be persecuted, and many have paid the price of a martyr's death for their loyalty to him. While you may not be asked to surrender your life in martyrdom, you may encounter opposition and persecution.

It sometimes happens that personal attacks are launched from within the immediate family when a person's life is turned over to the Lord. When I received my spiritual healing, I became a brand-new person. Friends, and even strangers, commented on my radiant glow. My family, however, was not comfortable with the dramatic changes they saw in me.

This was a challenging time for my marriage. My husband of twenty-four years complained that I was not the same woman he had married. He no longer knew me. Even as I coped with the physical threat of death from cancer, I could see that the old person I used to be was dying too. It was as though a new person stepped out of my cancerous shell.

The person I had always known myself to be, the person I was afraid others might not love, said, "I'm coming out. I will not be stifled any more!" While I certainly did not want to hurt those I loved, I knew I could not stuff the new self back inside. There was no map to guide me. I stumbled and fell a lot as I learned how to walk all over again.

YOU WILL BECOME A NEW CREATION

The Jesus Walk presents other problems. Some of your old relationships may no longer work. Your friends will feel self-conscious using bad language in your presence. You will feel discomfiture as well. What seemed right yesterday may not conform to the new person you are today.

You may also discover that your Christian moral values and your "resemblance" to Jesus are not welcome in the workplace. Not only are these values occasionally unwelcome, they can become a source of embarrassment for others. Profit, power, and personal gain are often valued more than human dignity, morality, and concern for others.

Immorality has found a comfortable niche in all levels of business and government. You not only need to weigh your own decisions, you have to decide how to react to the wrong choices of your peers. Such decisions are not always clear-cut and easy. Spiritual survival in a difficult world requires that you keep your eye on the prize, Jesus.

Jesus does not want to break up your family, nor does he want to take away your friends. He will, however, alter your relationships. Your sensitivity to the others in your life will help preserve your family stability and will safeguard your relationships. Just because you have "found Jesus" in a new and exciting way, doesn't mean you should coerce others to embrace him in the same way. Each person's walk with God is a delicate and private matter.

God wants your service. Others will see Jesus shining through you, like a radiant light. When they see your Christ-like kindness and compassion, they will want to imitate you. Let the unmistakable glow of Christ's peace in your eyes cause people to ask you for the secret. They will desire the same peace and joy for themselves. Reflecting to others the Christ who dwells within you is the best witness you can give.

You may be wondering how you will reach this wonderful state of Christ-centeredness. While it is true that spiritual growth is fed by grace, there are things you can do to cooperate with God's grace. Jesus wants to teach you but you must open the book. By reading Holy Scripture, you can learn how Jesus lived and loved. When you meditate on his teachings, he will give you insights into the ways his lessons directly apply to your life.

MARY SHOWS US HOW TO CARRY JESUS IN THE WORLD

You can learn to imitate Christ by contemplating the example of his mother. Imagine what thoughts went through the youthful virgin's mind when the angel Gabriel told her she would be overshadowed by the Holy Spirit and give birth to the Messiah. Even though there would be gossip and doubts about her virginity, she accepted this news with dignity and humility. Mary's "Yes" came from the deep well-spring of her faith in the Father and her readiness to obey him.

It was the infusion of the Holy Spirit that enabled Mary to maintain her commitment in faith. Mary knew that Joseph, a moral and responsible man, would have a difficult struggle with her news. Furthermore, a woman accused of unfaithfulness to her betrothed might be stoned to death. Joseph even considered divorcement to protect Mary's life. It was only after God sent reassurance through an angel that he was able to believe Mary's story and take her for his wife.

In spite of these concerns, Mary made a long journey to visit her cousin, Elizabeth, whose own child leapt in her womb at the sight of Mary. When Elizabeth confirmed the angel's message and welcomed the mother of the Messiah, Mary responded with modesty and humility. (Luke 1:46–49)

Mary shows us how to carry Jesus into the world with faith and humility. Life will present you with problems. You will be misunderstood. You may be disbelieved and mocked. You might feel embarrassment or shame over the actions of your family. Someone may treat you unlovingly, inventing lies that wound you deeply. People may gossip about you, or ridicule you for your faith and beliefs. You will be tempted to strike back, to loudly defend yourself, to vent your hurt and anger. Instead you can follow Mary's example.

How much better it is to draw upon the strength of God than to react in an ungodly way. Like Mary, we can accept embarrassments with grace. We can learn dignity from her.

Mary's modest response can be ours. It is the Lord who is great, not us. We are lowly servants who wait upon him. If we appear pious and perform holy deeds, it is only because of his presence within us. He does great and wonderful things for us, but it is only through his grace that we can do great things for him.

MARY WAS CHRIST-CENTERED

Not only will you be blessed as you serve the Lord, those who receive you as his ambassador will be equally blessed. (Mt 10:40–41) Jesus wants our service. He wants our minds, our hearts, our hands, our all. Just as Mary said her gracious "Yes" to God the Father, she continued to say yes by living her commitment. We see her submission and her servitude at every step of her journey with Christ.

Mary knew her place and showed restraint. Yet, she did not hesitate to ask Jesus to perform his first miracle at the Cana wedding. (Jn 2) She had deep faith. There was no doubt in her mind that he would grant her request. Mary was properly assertive, but never aggressive. Mary, who was at his side in Cana prompting him to launch his ministry, stayed with her Son as he proceeded toward the inevitable cross.

Mary was always there in the background, waiting to serve as she was needed. She must have comforted the people waiting their turn to be healed by Jesus. Imagine her walking among the crowds gathered, bringing a cup of water to a sick man lying on his mat, wiping the brow of a woman in pain. Perhaps she rocked cranky babies, calming them with a lullaby and giving their mothers a rest. Little children would have been drawn to her kind face and her gentle ways. She probably hugged them, told them stories, and made them laugh.

We see Mary's strength at the foot of the cross. (Jn 19:25–27) Jesus had been betrayed by a close friend. Imagine how her heart must have ached as the drama of the crucifixion unfolded! An ugly jeering crowd had demanded the death of Jesus. Soldiers had beaten him, pressed a crown of thorns into his head, and spat upon him in mockery. Her dear Son suffered physical pain and humiliating insults. He who had healed so many was judged to be worse than a common criminal.

As Jesus trudged up the hill to Golgotha, Mary must have walked in his footsteps. Who can describe the sorrow she felt as she watched the soldiers nail Jesus' body to the cross? What was she thinking as he hung there in pain and agony? This was the child she had carried in her womb. This was the boy she had lovingly raised. This was the man, the healer, the Messiah. No one on earth knew him as well as his mother.

In the depth of his agony on the cross, Jesus spoke to Mary. He who was in the act of surrendering everything to his heavenly Father, relinquished his own mother to John and to us. She is our spiritual mother. Mary models for us what it means to carry Christ in the world. In the stable at Bethlehem and at the foot of the cross, Mary had nothing, yet she had everything. She had Jesus.

Mary was Christ-centered in the truest sense. Her life is a powerful witness to the depth of her faith in God. Faith continued to sustain her as the Holy Spirit strengthened her, guiding her footsteps on the path laid out by Jesus. Even after the burial of her Son, Mary must have believed his promise that he would rise again on the third day.

THE EMPOWERMENT OF THE HOLY SPIRIT

After Jesus returned to his Father in heaven, Mary waited with the Apostles for empowerment by the Holy Spirit. Just as she had waited in prayerful anticipation to give birth to Jesus, Mary now waited in constant prayer for the birth of Christ's church. When the Holy Spirit came upon those gathered in the upper room, they received wisdom, understanding, fortitude, and all the other gifts they needed to carry Christ's Good News to others.

It is unlikely that the apostles foresaw themselves as evangelists and healers when they first decided to follow Jesus. The apostles initially followed him because they recognized the truth that he spoke. However, Jesus knew that he must continue to teach and prepare them for larger responsibilities. As their faith and understanding increased, the apostles grew ready to participate more fully in his ministry. When they preached the Good News that Jesus was the Savior, they saw many conversions. They also witnessed numerous physical cures when they prayed.

Jesus passed his torch of ministry to ordinary people. Through careful preparation and the gift of his Spirit, he provided his first disciples with all that they needed so that they could accomplish what ordinary people cannot. Jesus knew that it would require many people to spread his Word throughout the world.

Through the empowerment of the Holy Spirit, we too become workers for Christ, commissioned to spread the Good News. Jesus is inviting you to participate in his ministry. Should you accept his invitation, he will lead you in the way he wants you to follow him. Be prepared for surprises. You may envision your ministry one way, while Jesus has a totally different plan for you.

When God commissions you to serve in ministry, he bestows gifts that are complimentary to your personality. He will make the best use of your strengths to carry out this work.

Before his conversion, Saul was a persecutor of Christians. He became Paul the Apostle, an ardent proclaimer of Christ's Good News of salvation. Jesus transformed him from worst enemy to best friend, utilizing Paul's special gifts of fierce loyalty and unrelenting dedication to work for good. Though not one of the original apostles, Paul was singled out by Jesus to spread Christianity to the Gentiles. He was as zealous in this work as he previously had been in persecuting Christians.

God, who knows your strengths and weaknesses, also knows your potential for growth. He may stretch you in new directions. When Jeremiah was called by God to be a prophet, he protested that he was a mere boy and unworthy of that assignment. Yahweh corrected him, saying, "There! I am putting words in your mouth." (Jer 1:9) In obedience, Jeremiah cooperated with God's grace by opening his mouth and allowing Yahweh to speak through him. He fulfilled his commitment in spite of persecution and personal problems.

JESUS WANTS TO EMPOWER YOU

When you are open to serving Jesus, you will put your self-interests aside and submit to God's direction. There will be times when you doubt you can fulfil his demands. You may even want to argue with his directions. In the end, however, submission is the answer.

When I received the spiritual healing shortly after my cancer diagnosis, I felt as though I was on a honeymoon. I had learned how much the Father loved me and I basked in the comfort of that love! I thought that nothing more was expected of me. Then when I received my sudden miracle, I was initially plagued with doubts.

While I knew I should feel joyful and happy, I worried that my cancer might return. I went to Father Dennis Steik for advice. It had been two weeks since my miracle and decisions had to be made about my treatments. I didn't know what to do and I wondered what to tell people who knew I had been dying. In spite of Father's reassurances that I had received a miracle, I left his office in tears.

Meanwhile, I met a woman who was scheduled for a biopsy. She was sure she had a recurrence of breast cancer. When we said goodbye, I clumsily grabbed Faye's shoulder, saying, "I will be praying for you." I had promised to visit her in the hospital but I received a phone call telling me not to come. Her lump was gone! My own miracle had astonished me. Now I was bewildered. Since Faye and I had the same surgeon, I questioned him. He explained that there had been no reason to admit her for a biopsy because the lump had completely vanished. "I don't have any explanation," he said, "but it is definitely gone!"

When I returned to Father Dennis with this news, it was apparent to him that the woman had been healed through my prayers and my touch. "Where does this come from?" I asked. "I don't like it. It scares me."

Father Dennis explained that healing comes from God and perhaps Jesus wanted me to have a healing ministry. I felt shaken. I could not even imagine myself in such a role. As we talked, I recalled the words I had spoken to Father Dennis at the healing service. Just before he anointed me and prayed over me, I had said, "You know what needs healing…but I also ask that God will use me as an instrument of healing in the lives of others." Those words had sounded strange to me when I first spoke them. They sounded even stranger now.

Father Dennis explained that God often uses people to bring healing in the same areas where they have been healed. That probably explained the sudden disappearance of Faye's lump. I had touched her and prayed for her and Jesus had answered my prayer. He encouraged me to go through the doors God opened before me, trusting that God would show me what to do. He said that if I continued to say "Yes!" to the Lord, without questioning and without reservation, then God would continue to increase his gifts to me.

After several hours of gentle persuasion, Father Dennis convinced me that God was calling me to ministry. I remember the surrender in my voice as I said, "God has been so good to me. If this is what he wants, how can I refuse?" In a small room on a college campus, I said my own "Yes" to the Lord. Yes, I would pray over people. Yes, I would go without hesitation through every door he opened before me. Yes, I would do whatever he asked me to do.

In order for you to accept the invitation God wants to give you, you must hear his call. Have you ever driven through the car wash and forgotten to return your radio antenna to its correct position? The car radio is on and properly tuned, but no sound is coming through. Or worse yet, you can hear nothing but loud static. Well, in order for Jesus to speak to your heart you must be prepared and you must listen.

Mary was prepared because she knew the old prophecies. Her people were awaiting the Messiah. The words of the Magnificat, which she spoke to Elizabeth, reveal her familiarity with the Old Testament Psalms, as well with phrases from Isaiah and others. You can prepare for ministry by familiarizing yourself with God's words in Holy Scripture. When you know his Word, you will be better equipped to recognize his voice.

Mary was probably in quiet prayer when the angel Gabriel spoke to her. It is difficult to hear God's voice amidst the noise and distractions of modern life. Your decision to spend time in silent prayer is a good first step toward hearing the voice of God in your heart. If you are willing to turn your life over to the Lord, you must be alert and prepared to hear and answer his call.

BECOMING CHRIST-CENTERED

During the forty days after his resurrection from the dead, Jesus continued teaching and preparing his apostles to carry on his work. Before leaving, he commissioned them to go forth to all nations, baptizing and teaching as he had done. He further promised that he would send his Spirit. They waited obediently in prayer for his Spirit to descend upon them and equip them for ministry.

Are you ready and willing to learn so that you can work for Jesus? Everything you need to know has already been given to you in Holy Scripture, but in order to learn you must open the book and read. By spending time reflecting and praying on Scripture, you will begin to hear his directions for your life.

Read Jeremiah 17:7–8. Are you like the tree he describes, with its roots watered by the stream, always verdant and perpetually bearing fruit?

Read Matthew 25:1–13. In the parable, ten bridesmaids awaited the arrival of the bridegroom. Five had sufficient oil for their lamps but the other five were unprepared. When the bridegroom arrived, the foolish bridesmaids were out shopping for oil!

Read Jeremiah 18:1–6. Yahweh sent Jeremiah to the potter's house to watch him work. When a vessel did not turn out right, the potter reshaped the clay into a new vessel.

What kind of a vessel are you? Does God want to reshape you? Are there rough edges that need to be smoothed? Are you so full that there is no room for God? Are you so empty of God's word that he does not find a place there? Are you prepared to receive the Holy Spirit? What can you do to get ready?

Jesus gave us a role model for living the Christ-centered life. Meet her in the following meditation:

Meditation:

Who is this Mary, our Mother? Pretend you are walking on holy ground and suddenly, in the crowd, you notice a gentle, quiet woman. She approaches you, reaching out her hand in a gesture of friendship. You recognize Mary from the many paintings and statues you have seen. Who is this woman, really? What do you see? Look into her eyes. Do you see a mirror reflection of Jesus, her Son? What advice does she have for you?

7. Just Say Yes!

"...you will receive power...." (Acts 1:8)

The power and the presence of the Holy Spirit is not new but it is probably the least understood attribute of God. Before the resurrected Christ ascended to his Father, he instructed his apostles:

> And now I am sending down to you what the Father has promised. Stay in the city then, until you are clothed with the power from on high. (Lk 24:49)

Immediately after the crucifixion, the followers of Jesus waited in Jerusalem, as they had been told. Since the murderous spirit that had led to Christ's crucifixion was not a favorable climate for spreading the Good News, the apostles prayed together in the upper room, along with Mary the Mother of Jesus and several others. Finally, on Pentecost the Holy Spirit descended upon them in tongues of fire, bestowing special gifts or charisms.

Filled with the Holy Spirit, they spoke with the charismatic gift of speech to a crowd of people gathered outside. People from many different nations understood them, each in their own language. Declaring that Jesus Christ was truly the Messiah, Peter called upon the people to repent, to receive baptism and forgiveness of their sins, and to receive the Holy Spirit.

> The promise that was made is for you and your children, and for all those who are far away, for all those whom the Lord our God will call to himself. (Acts 2:39)

Before the crucifixion, Peter's fear had caused him to deny knowing Jesus. Now empowered by the Holy Spirit, Peter courageously stepped forward to lead Christ's church. Jesus had commissioned the apostles to evangelize the world, but it was only through his Spirit that they were able to fulfill their mission.

With bold proclamations that Jesus is God, they greatly increased the numbers of the early Christian community. Like Jesus, they also healed the sick, cast out demons, and performed miracles. Simple men were able to do wondrous things through the power of the Spirit. In spite of threats and persecution, the apostles continued their mission.

> ...you will receive power when the Holy Spirit comes on you, and then you will be my witnesses not only in Jerusalem but throughout Judaea and Samaria, and indeed to the ends of the earth. (Acts 1:8)

Early Doctors of the Church taught that the charisms were meant for everyone, not just for a few.[21] The gifts of the Holy Spirit are not the property of an elite group. They are part of our heritage as children of the Father and disciples of Jesus. The charismatic gifts, imparted through Baptism in the Holy Spirit, are available to everyone too.

THE HOLY SPIRIT RENEWS GOD'S PEOPLE

Around the beginning of the 20th century, a new era of the Holy Spirit dawned in the United States. A pentecostal revival started around the turn of the century and gained impetus in the early 1900's in Los Angeles. The Catholic charismatic movement began to flourish in the 1960's when a group of Duquesne University students experienced the power of the Holy Spirit. This movement has continued to spread to more than 100 countries throughout the world.

The Holy Spirit is renewing the Church and working to bring unity to God's people. The Holy Spirit is active in large denominations as well as in smaller, less well-known congregations. The Spirit is also the source of spiritual awakening, grace, and sanctification for God's people.

Even though I had received the sacrament of Confirmation as a child, I had never fully realized the spiritual gifts I received. With that sacrament, the tiny flame of faith implanted at Baptism is meant to quicken into a blazing fire, strengthening faith and challenging the recipient to use the gifts of the Holy Spirit in a bold way. Often, these gifts remain dormant until a new infusion of the Holy Spirit wakens the soul and stirs it to action.

Spirit Baptism animates the soul and creates a hunger for God's word. Quietly and unexpectedly, I received this baptism at the same time as my spiritual healing, when I confessed my life and turned it over to Jesus. He created in me a deep longing to know God's word, along with the desire to walk more closely with him. This was accompanied by an insatiable yearning to serve him.

Baptism in the Spirit often occurs through the "laying on of hands," a form of prayer that originated in the early church. After Philip preached the Good News and worked miracles in a Samarian town, the Samaritan people turned their lives over to Jesus. Then Peter and John went to visit them.

> ...they went down there, and prayed for the Samaritans to receive the Holy Spirit, for as yet he had not come down on any of them: they had only been baptised in the name of the Lord Jesus. Then they laid hands on them, and they received the Holy Spirit. (Acts 8:14–17)

The person who receives prayers for Spirit Baptism makes a commitment to serve the Lord and in doing so, exhibits a willingness to receive special gifts of the Holy Spirit. Just as gifts accompany the sacrament of Confirmation, spiritual charisms are given with this new infusion of God's Spirit. All of these are bestowed by the Holy Spirit, "...who distributes different gifts to different people just as he chooses." (1 Cor 12:11) These are special favors from a loving God.

> ...we have received the Spirit that comes from God, to teach us to understand the gifts that he has given us. (1 Cor 2:12)

The charisms have no value until they are used. If you have tried wilderness camping, you know that freeze-dried foods, though lightweight and easy to carry, are unpalatable in their packaged form. They require water, heat, and careful stirring before they are palatable. Similarly, your walk with Jesus requires the living water of his Spirit poured out upon you. Fired by the love of the Spirit and stirred by his energy, you walk arm and arm with Jesus.

The Father sent Jesus, his Word, to redeem us. Jesus gives us his very breath, the Spirit, to teach and inspire us. The three Persons of God are inseparable. Your spiritual life cannot be divorced from the Spirit because it is Christ's own Spirit that brings you into relationship with God. His Spirit nourishes your prayer life, and prepares you for your final journey to the bosom of God.

If you reject the Holy Spirit, you reject the Father and Jesus. However, the Holy Spirit will not force gifts upon you. Refusing the gifts offered by the Spirit is like dipping into a well but not reaching deeply enough to touch the water. You will remain empty and frustrated.

> An unspiritual person is one who does not accept anything of the Spirit of God: he sees it all as nonsense; it is beyond his understanding because it can only be understood by means of the Spirit. (1 Cor 2:14)

THE CALL TO CHRISTIAN COMMUNITY

St. Paul reminds us that the charisms that accompany Spirit Baptism are intended to help us establish the kingdom of God on earth. Just as the apostles remained faithful to prayer and community as they organized Christ's Church under the direction of God's own Spirit, we are meant to use the charisms to build up the Church.

Because the charisms of the Holy Spirit are interrelated, we are encouraged to use them in community. They are not given to elevate one person above others. The charismatic gifts are meant to be used in harmony and with humility. Paul reminds us that love is the highest and most important gift of all. Without it, the other gifts are worthless. (1 Cor 13)

The Spirit gives you charisms that are complementary to your personality. The same God who knitted you together in your mother's womb knows your capabilities. God uses people in ways that utilize their existing talents and strengths. Since there are numerous gifts, there are appropriate gifts for everyone. Whatever gifts you receive, be thankful to the Giver for drawing you into ministry and trust that he will supply your needs.

The special charism I received from the Holy Spirit was the gift to pray for healing. When I first received it, I felt very unsure of myself. After I said "Yes" to the Lord, I struggled with "How?" Nothing in my traditional prayer life had prepared me to pray over others for healing. My prayers had always been read from books or recited from memory. Now I had to learn to pray aloud in my own words.

When I stepped out in faith and asked God to heal others, my first attempts felt awkward. All of this was new to me. Initially, I practiced on my thirteen-year-old son. Whenever he had a headache or a scrape (there were many), I prayed over him. He was a willing subject and my confidence grew as those prayers for little healings were answered.

JESUS MINISTERS THROUGH YOU

God quickly showed me that when I opened my mouth to pray, he would help me. I also learned that the words I said were not nearly as important as the intention of my heart. God knew that I wanted people to be relieved of their suffering and he answered my prayers even when my words sounded inadequate to me. Jesus never asks us to do more than we are able, but through his grace we can do more than we ever thought we could.

Jesus also provided me with sound instruction. The priests who had prayed for my healing also encouraged and shepherded me. When Father Dennis asked me to accompany him to the hospital to visit patients, I learned from his sensitive manner and his gentle way of praying.

Jesus uses our love and compassion for the sick to change people's lives and heal them. Even when my words of prayer sound inept to my ears, Jesus speaks through me and tells the person exactly he wants them to hear. It is Jesus who heals. He merely uses our hands and our prayers, our love and our compassion, to accomplish his healing.

In the early days of my ministry, I stumbled a lot but Jesus held me up and guided me. He still does. Of the many charismatic gifts, I had only love, compassion, and healing. I felt like a baby charismatic. There was so much to be learned but I was also busy raising my large family. My chemotherapy treatments were ongoing and my daughter's mental problems continued. Life was very full!

That summer, I spent five days each week at a radiation treatment center. This provided me with relief from family problems and for the first time in years I had time to myself. Since the cancer had already disappeared in February, I considered this a vacation. I thought perhaps God placed me in an apartment building filled with cancer patients so that I could pray over them. While I did pray *for* them, there was never an opportunity to pray *over* them.

The person that Jesus brought across my path that summer was a friend from my grade school days. We had not seen each other for years but she was living less than a mile from my treatment center. The summer passed quickly as we renewed the bond of our friendship. She was in pain over a failed marriage, and I was the one God had sent to comfort and support her through a painful divorce. Because his Spirit came to help me and provided the needed gifts, my compassion deepened and I learned to be a better listener.

One of the first gifts often given by the Spirit is the language of speech, or tongues. This gift flows naturally for some, while others struggle with it. I was so uneasy about tongues, I had read several books on the subject trying to understand it. My apprehension about this charism prevented me from attending the charismatic prayer meetings.

THE SPIRIT IS A GENTLE TEACHER

That summer, I met Bob and Judith. She was a dynamic Jewish woman and also a writer. Because Bob was undergoing radiation treatment for a brain tumor, they were interested in my miracle. They asked if Father Dennis would pray over them and I arranged for them to come to the Sunday evening charismatic Mass, which was held outdoors during the summer.

At the end of the liturgy, Father Dennis called the couple forward and we all gathered around them in prayer. When I heard what I thought were the voices of angels filling the night air with song, I opened my eyes wide. People all around me were singing in tongues. The sound was so melodic and beautiful, my apprehension quickly vanished.

Even though my nervousness about the gift of tongues had been overcome, I continued to postpone my first visit to a prayer meeting. I had promised to take my daughter, but when the day arrived I said I was too tired. She chided me, "Mom, it doesn't matter if you are tired. All you have to do is sit there!"

In spite of my reluctance to be there, Jesus snagged my heart and drew me in. Sensitive to the discomfort of newcomers, Father Dennis opened the prayer meeting with a brief explanation of the gifts of the Spirit. I sat by the door so I could sneak out at any time but God had a different plan. During that evening, tears streamed down my face as Jesus gently lifted away burdens. I did not know what was being healed but my fear was taken away and I never again wanted to miss a prayer meeting.

There are many different charismatic gifts and while they should be used in love, it is important to remember that God is a God of order. (1 Cor 14:33) He gives you the gifts you need but he expects you to use them with common sense and sensitivity. Tongues is a prayer language between you and God. If you stand babbling in tongues at a busy intersection, you will attract ridicule, not souls for the Lord. While this is an extreme example, it demonstrates that there is a proper time and place for everything.

Prophecy is a message of inspiration, spoken to your heart by the Holy Spirit. With this gift you have opportunities to build up the prayer community by sharing what the Lord tells you. This gift is not the Lord's authorization to tell your family and friends what *you* think they should be doing. As long as you remember the Source and the purpose of the gifts, you will not misuse them.

I learned more about the charisms at the weekly prayer meetings, which fueled the power of the Holy Spirit within me. Months earlier I had said my "Yes" to the Lord. Now I plunged forward into the Lord's arms with a big "Amen!" From that moment forward, my spiritual energy increased.

At a Life in the Spirit retreat, I heard a call to reach out with open arms and embrace the Lord. Gradually another hang-up was taken away. While I longed to open my heart, mind, and will to his presence, I still had difficulty yielding. When I tried to raise my arms as others did during the singing at Mass, the best I could manage was to sit with my palms turned upward in my lap. In this posture, I prayed that I might be an empty cup for Jesus to fill and use, and I asked Jesus to take away my self-consciousness.

Then, when we sang the Amen during Mass, I began to clap and suddenly I saw this simple gesture of clapping in a new light. Rather than an action of bringing my hands together in a joyful rhythm, I saw it as a need to push my arms apart, to open them wider to receive God's loving embrace. I began to relax in his presence.

Like a sponge, I soaked up teachings on the Holy Spirit. During prayers for the Baptism of the Holy Spirit, retreat teams asked Jesus to enhance his Spirit's gifts in each person's life. Since I had already received Spirit Baptism and the gift of healing, I asked for the gift of discernment to guide my prayers for healing.

Not everyone experiences the apprehension that I initially felt over the special gifts. I remember one friend who came to her first prayer meeting in a spirit of total openness. While we were singing songs of praise, she felt on fire from head to toe and began singing in tongues. She received an instantaneous Spirit Baptism.

OPENNESS TO GOD'S SPIRIT

Are you are open to the Baptism of the Holy Spirit and the reception of charisms? If so, perhaps you are wondering what to do next. God, who knows your heart, is already drawing you more deeply into relationship. Ask him for guidance. Is there someone in your church who prays with charismatic gifts? If not, try to locate a spirit-filled prayer group. Jesus wants to fill you with his Spirit.

If you are unable to locate an established group, perhaps God is calling you to begin one. You can gather together friends who share your interest in a deeper, more committed walk with Jesus. As you meet for prayer and scripture, acting on the inner prompts from the Spirit, he will enlighten and fill you. He will not disappoint you.

> Ask, and it will be given to you; search, and you will find; knock, and the door will be opened to you. For the one who asks always receives; the one who searches always finds; the one who knocks will always have the door opened to him... (Mt 7:7–8)

The Father knows you better than you know yourself. He knows about your many needs and he sent his Son to heal your sickness and your sorrows. Jesus wants a conversion, a transformation of your heart. One day, he will ask what you did to bring his love and peace into the world. Jesus is calling you now. He calls his children to pray together and to minister to one another. He is offering you his Spirit.

Baptism in the Holy Spirit results from a decision to move into deeper relationship with God. It is a heart experience, as opposed to intellectual knowledge of God. The Spirit says, "Come with faith. Come and pray. Praise God. Let me quicken the fire within you. Let me sanctify your heart and fill you with gifts. The answer is easy. Just say yes, and I will do the rest."

† † †

CHANGING ROADBLOCKS INTO BUILDING BLOCKS

The Spirit of God offers you special gifts but he will not force them upon you. Acceptance of the charisms is a matter of choice. God never takes away your free will. Are you open to receiving gifts that the Holy Spirit offers you?

An Examen:

- Do you hear Jesus calling you to a new life in him?
- Is there something that stands between you and saying "Yes"?
- Make a list of your priorities.
- Spend time contemplating your priorities.
- What unnecessary acts do you perform simply out of habit?
- What can you delete without backing away from moral responsibilities?
- What position does Jesus occupy on your list?
- Do you have a plan for your life or just let it happen?
- Is service to the Lord something you plan to do later?
- List the roadblocks that prevent you from saying "Yes" to the Lord today.
- Pray about your roadblocks.

Read and reflect upon the following scriptures, which describe the Holy Spirit and charisms: Mt 3:11, 1 Cor 12:1–30, Acts 2:1–13, Eph 4:9–13, 1 Cor 13:1–17.

An Interactive Story: (You choose the ending)
You receive an invitation. The King announces a fabulous give-away. He has decided to share the royal treasures with some of his loyal followers. You are among those chosen. You line up with others in the village square to receive a gift.

Some of the packages are large. Others are small. Your eyes are attracted to a beautiful red-and-gold box that you hope to receive. You hold your breath. You watch as one by one, the packages are distributed by the King. When you reach the front of the line, you sigh with relief. Your box is still there. No one has taken it.

You smile eagerly at the King and reach out your hand toward the box you have been admiring. The King smiles broadly at you and hands you a plainly wrapped box. "This is a very special gift I have chosen for you," he says. "Use it well." The red-and-gold box is not for you.

Ending 1. You are disappointed. While others happily unwrap their gifts, you slip away unnoticed and return home. You put the unopened gift box in the attic, flop in your easy chair, and turn on the television to search for a diversion.

Ending 2. Initially, you feel disappointed, but you smile graciously and accept the gift you are given. The King, a wise and kind and generous man, chose this gift especially for you. Trusting in his judgement, you carefully open the plain box. You aren't sure how to use this gift, but you admire it gratefully. Then you read the instructions. You want to be sure to use it well.

8. What Would Jesus Say?

"How happy are the poor in spirit;…"
(Mt 5:3)

*W*hen Jesus infuses you with his Spirit, you begin to open up, like a flower extending its petals to the warmth of the sun. The Holy Spirit freshens the air and sweeps away your complacency. He also puts a burden on your conscience and draws you into service for the Lord. (Rom 12:9–13)

You may be wondering how you can possibly respond to this call to service. Perhaps you prefer your life just the way it is. Change implies risk, but the Holy Spirit always brings change. Service flows out of a Spirit-filled life because the greatest gift of the Spirit is love, and love is something that you do.

When you accept the gifts of the Spirit and welcome Jesus into your heart, he doesn't just come inside and settle down for a nap. He plans to use you to accomplish his work. Whatever you are asked to do, you are not expected to do it alone. When Jesus opens a door, he also provides a way. Jesus, who walks with you, empowers you through his Spirit to step out in faith and use the charisms. All that is required is your trusting cooperation. Jesus chose you and he calls you to bear fruit as his disciple. (Jn 15:16)

Jesus describes himself as the true Vine and his Father as the Vinedresser, who cuts away every branch that does not bear fruit. He urges us to stay close to the Vine, in order to bear much fruit and give glory to the Father. (Jn 15) If we are to cling to the Vine and bear fruit, we must have an affinity for the Vine. We must become like it in every way. Jesus wants us to be so much like him that we adapt our lives to his values, his love, his compassion, and his precepts.

JESUS WAS A SERVANT LEADER

Jesus was not an elitist, he was a servant leader. His ministry took him into the midst of the lowly, the poor, and the sinners. This made him a constant target of criticism by the Pharisees. However, Jesus did not mingle with the lowly in order to be like them. Rather he spent time with them so that they could learn to be like him.

Jesus walked among ordinary people touching, consoling, healing, and setting their hearts on fire with love for his Father. He touched sinners and hypocrites, lepers and prostitutes, beggars and thieves. Jesus was a radical whose teachings reflect a dramatic departure from traditional thinking. Our Messiah's way is not the way of the world.

Jesus not only preached love, he revealed love by forgiving and healing the little ones. Those who walked in his presence knew the love of the Father, because Jesus proclaimed love. Jesus was also a well-balanced man. He loved life and he loved people. He mingled with people, shared food and drink with them, listened to their problems, helped them, cured them, and taught them.

> …This is my commandment:
> love one another,
> as I have loved you. (Jn 15:12)

His commandment summarizes all that Jesus taught. More is expected of you under the new standard. You are told to turn the other cheek, to go the extra mile, to give to anyone who asks, to pray for persecutors, and to love your enemies. (Mt 5) Jesus speaks clearly, leaving no doubt about his meaning. Jesus knows exactly where he is taking you. He promises the kingdom but he also commands love and care for his little ones. Entrance to the kingdom carries a price.

JESUS' RADICAL CHALLENGE OF LOVE

We often find it is easier and more natural to love those in our immediate circle than to love God's little ones. Sometimes we prefer to keep our distance and maintain our ignorance of their situations. Yet, if we believe what Jesus taught, these are the brothers and sisters whom we must love. The poor are down-trodden and destitute. They rely on us because they lack means of their own.

Poverty isn't eliminated by a hot meal or a Christmas food basket. It continues all year long, all over the world. Poverty affects orphans and starving families in Third World countries, as well as the hungry who reside invisibly in your own neighborhood. A new breed of poverty is developing as large numbers of productive people lose jobs and homes when their companies downsize. Meanwhile, government budget cuts slash away at the meager benefits of the poor.

What would Jesus say about these situations? Time and again, you will ask this question as you walk his walk.

Dearest to the heart of Jesus are the poor and lowly. He befriended prostitutes and criminals, forgiving their sins. He healed the sick, the disabled, and the terminally ill. Jesus preached the Good News to the poor. To the spiritually separated, he offered hope and encouragement.

Jesus loves the outcasts of society. Today, he wants you to walk with him among the poor and the homeless. He wants you to reach out to the chemically addicted, to the winos in the gutter, and to the addicts in needle park. He is equally concerned about the plight of illegal aliens and the lives of murderers on death row. Jesus calls on you to comfort widows and orphans, battered women and abused children. Jesus wants you to bring his love to them.

Jesus wants you to reach out to all who are separated in society. He who healed the lepers wants you to bring Christ's compassion to homosexuals and to others who are dying of AIDS. Forgotten people in mental institutions need to receive God's word. He wants you to pray for aborted babies and to be present in a loving way when their parents suffer latent anguish for their lost babies. His little ones need someone to listen with compassion and to tell them that God loves them.

Old people wither away in nursing homes, forgotten by their families and ignored by the outside world. They slump in their wheelchairs or lie helplessly in beds. Their spirits may languish for a loving touch, a smile, a pat on the hand. If only someone would read to them, or write a letter for them, now that their hands are shaky and their eyes are dim.

Mentally impaired people in institutions are real people with real feelings, who respond warmly to love and kindness. There are so many little ones and while their circumstances vary greatly, they all share one characteristic. They are vulnerable.

Those who live a hand-to-mouth existence, perhaps with a roof overhead and a small paycheck, are just a heartbeat away from disaster. Just one serious illness or accident can wipe out their small sustenance.

Even more vulnerable are people who live on the street. We see the homeless everywhere and we are no longer surprised or curious. Our eyes and our hearts have grown immune to their plight. Couples with children in tow form caravans with their shopping baskets and wagons. Where are they going? What do they eat? Where do they sleep? Do the nomad children go to school and learn to read? How do these families protect themselves against criminal violence?

Look in your Bible. Where do you find Jesus? He is walking among the marginal people. A margin is the outside limit or edge. Many little ones live on the edge of society. Margin also means the limit below which economic activity cannot be continued under normal circumstances. Marginal means situated at a border and located at the fringe of consciousness.[22]

The little ones are at the fringes of our awareness. They are transparent. When we look at them, we look right through them. Perhaps we avoid seeing them because their plight is too painful to comprehend. We may feel helpless to solve their problems. We may imagine ourselves in the same condition of poverty, and withdraw from them in fear.

Marginal people live at the extremity of society. That which is normal for average people is not the norm for the disadvantaged. Some have an existence so far below the normal standard that employment and self-help are out of the question. Preventive medical and dental care are denied them. All of the little ones have needs, and their most desperate need is love. The touch of Jesus is missing from their lives. They have no hope for tomorrow.

WHERE ARE YOU IN THIS PICTURE?

The term "God's little ones" includes you and me, even though we may not live in institutions, suffer addictions, or live on the margins of society. Are we not all wounded to some extent? Have you never mourned the death of a loved one? Have you never felt persecuted, either at home, at school, or in the workplace? Perhaps in your own church? Has your own family been devoid of problems such as alcoholism, divorce, or financial setbacks? Even those comfortable with material possessions can be broken people.

We are all wounded to some extent. Because we inherit the biological imperfections of our ancestors, our genes may carry the seeds of incurable diseases. Emotionally, we are the products of dysfunctional families. We live in a broken, troubled world. Spiritually, we all become alienated by sin, which is a turning away from God.

Just think about the problems we confront on a daily basis. We have hurts from the past, perhaps reaching back into early childhood. Our relationships are troubled. Sickness and worry are part of our daily struggle. Some are sandwiched between two needy generations, supporting children in college while caring for elderly parents. Our world is so full of pain and stress, and everyday there are new problems.

We worry about the threats of cancer and heart attacks, as well as Alzheimer's and AIDS. Will we survive on the highway? Are our children safe on the streets? Do they have good companions? Will they use drugs? Will they get into serious trouble? Can we afford to send them through college? Will they stay faithful to their religion? If not, will they return to God someday?

People are lashing out against one another. Respect for life and human dignity is vanishing. Our environment is polluted with chemicals, as well as with crime. Communities have become war zones, frequented by gang violence, drive-by shootings, rape, and murder. There are global problems of famine, terrorist attacks, war, genocide, and the threat of nuclear destruction. Who can ignore all this?

YOU NEED SOMEONE YOU CAN TRUST

You have all of these problems bombarding you and stealing your peace of mind. Perhaps you feel like a juggler with one hand tied behind your back, trying to keep all the balls in the air. These burdens make you very tired. They drain your energy. You need comfort. You need rest. You need someone to trust, someone who will say, "I understand. I want to help you." You need someone who will remove the heavy load and fill your heart with peace.

That someone is Jesus. He longs to comfort you. He wants you to trust him. He wants to take away your burdens. He wants to bring his peace to your heart. Jesus knows what it means to have problems. When he lived on earth, people did not understand him. Some of his own disciples fell asleep when he was most in need of their prayers and support.

Jesus suffered more than most of us ever will. Betrayed by a close friend, he was tortured, spat upon, jeered at, and he died a horrible death. Most of his followers were so fearful for their own safety, they abandoned him as he hung on the cross. Yes, Jesus knew physical pain, loneliness, abandonment, exhaustion, and mental anguish. Because he suffered everything that we suffer in our lives, he understands our troubles and our grief. We are afraid and he wants to alleviate our fears.

> Come to me, all you who labour and are overburdened, and
> I will give you rest. Shoulder my yoke and learn from me,
> for I am gentle and humble in heart, and you will find rest
> for your souls. Yes, my yoke is easy and my burden light.
> (Mt 11:28–30)

The Beatitudes are Jesus' message of love for his precious broken people. He who has great compassion for us wants us to show compassion to others. Since he said that the first will be last and the last first, it is no surprise that the "poor in spirit" are at the top of Christ's list. To these he promises the kingdom of heaven. The term "poor in spirit" broadens the boundaries of poverty to include anyone and everyone, regardless of their material circumstances. How can you be poor in spirit?

> I tell you solemnly, unless you change and become like little children you will never enter the kingdom of heaven.
>
> (Mt 18:3)

WHAT IS JESUS ASKING OF US?

Jesus calls us to be vulnerable like little children, who must depend upon adults to provide them with love and the basic necessities of life. Jesus wants us to rely totally on him. He wants us to put our hands in his and trust him to provide for all our needs. This is the poverty of spirit required for entrance into the kingdom.

We also become little when we learn to detach ourselves from our many worldly comforts. By allowing ourselves to live detached from the world and attached to Jesus, our lives become entwined with the less fortunate little ones. When a young man from a well-to-do family asked Jesus what was required so that he could enter the kingdom, he did not like the answer. Even though he had led a good life in obedience to the commandments, Jesus wanted greater sacrifice.

> There is still one thing you lack. Sell all that you own and distribute the money to the poor, and you will have treasure in heaven; then come, follow me. (Lk 18:22)

Jesus does not want our material possessions. He wants detachment from worldly things. He wants poverty of spirit. He wants us to exchange our selfish complacency for a spirit of generosity. If you have been richly blessed, you are expected to bless others out of your abundance. (Lk 12)

When Jesus returns in glory to ask your response to the Beatitudes, people from the beginning of time will be sorted, as sheep are separated from goats by the shepherd.

> Come, you whom my Father has blessed, take for your heritage the kingdom prepared for you since the foundation of the world. For I was hungry and you gave me food; I was thirsty and you gave me drink; I was a stranger and you

made me welcome; naked and you clothed me, sick and you
visited me, in prison and you came to see me…I tell you
solemnly, in so far as you did this to one of the least of these
brothers of mine, you did it to me. (Mt 25:34–36 and 40)

When you are inside the mind and heart of Jesus, with Jesus
dwelling inside your mind and heart, your heart becomes like
his. You begin to see Jesus everywhere. You find him in the sick,
in the broken, and in the homeless. You see others with new
eyes, because you see them through his eyes. When someone
treats you badly, you find it easier to forgive. You are compassionate even toward your enemies because they do not yet know
the fullness of Jesus' love.

Jesus will bring needy people across your path. He knows
when he places them there that you will not step on them. You
will be uncomfortable looking the other way and detouring
around them. You won't turn you back on them because you will
not turn your back on Jesus.

It is impossible to turn your back on Jesus when he is right
there at your side, holding onto you. Believe that he knows
where he is leading you. Trust Jesus to carry your burdens as
you walk with him. He wants your hands to be empty so that
you can reach out to help others.

Someone is hungry. Someone thirsts. Someone is in pain.
Someone is lonely. Someone is alienated. Someone is saying, "Is
that any of my business?" What would Jesus say?

Give, and there will be gifts for you: a full measure, pressed
down, shaken together, and running over, will be poured
into your lap; because the amount you measure out is the
amount you will be given back. (Lk 6:38)

Jesus tells us to clothe the naked with love and care, to shelter the homeless with dignity, and to embrace the alienated with
respect. Jesus tells us to give drink to the thirsty and food to the
hungry. The Beatitudes are his message of love for his precious
broken people. Think of them as the "BE attitudes." They
describe the attitude of love that we are called to be. We are
called to be eucharist, sharing ourselves as Jesus taught us and
quenching their thirst with the living water of his word.

† † †

REASSESSING YOUR VALUES

The ministry of Jesus was radical. He walked among the poor, the sick, the broken, and criminals. Above all, he cherished little children and asked us to become like them in spirit. Jesus shows us a new way of looking at the world. He urges us to find him in the downtrodden, in the little ones. Jesus wants to heal your eyes so that you will see and love others as he does.

Read Isaiah 61:1 and Matthew 25:31–45. What good news will you share with the poor? Will you be at Jesus' right hand?

Read Luke 15:8–10. What value do you put on a penny? Would you bend over to pick up a penny from the sidewalk? Try to think of ways that pennies can make a difference in the world.

Author William Saroyan shared this advice from an uncle, "Once a year, throw some money away." To prevent money from becoming a tyrant, he scattered several dollars worth of coins every year, and watched as people found them.[23] If you don't let go of money, it won't let go of you.

Try to imagine what it would be like to be homeless. The homeless have a lot. They have:
>No place to hang a hat.
>No hat to hang.
>No closet.
>No clothes to hang in the closet.
>No place to bathe.
>No bed to sleep in.
>No mailbox.
>No pantry or refrigerator.
>No place to belong.
>No regular income.
>No community except the homeless.
>The love and mercy of Jesus.

If you were President, how would you help the homeless?
If you were Jesus, what would you tell your church?

Meditation: The Widow's Mite

Imagine yourself in this scene: The temple hall is busy. Wealthy pharisees parade in and make a great show of their donations. You stand near the door, clutching two small coins. They are all that you own. Your clothes are shabby. You feel the paving stones through the worn spots of your shoes. After the crowd disperses, you quietly walk to the coin box and drop in your coins. You turn to leave and see Jesus standing there. What does Jesus say? How do you feel?

Read Isaiah 58:6–12 and Matthew 22:37–40. Through the prophet Isaiah, the Lord tells us what to do. Matthew gives us a summary in the two commandments of Jesus. To summarize further, you only need to remember four letters: L-O-V-E.

The final exam will be simple. There are only two commandments to know and two words. Engrave the words of the commandments on your heart. Learn the two words:

Love—something you do

Gospel—something you live

9. Come to the Vineyard

*"I am the true vine,
and my father is the vinedresser."*
(Jn 15:1)

A vine is a special type of plant because of the way it grows.
The main plant generates many branches and each has the
potential for extensive growth. The branches derive their
strength from a healthy vine. They are reliant on the vine
because without it, they cannot survive. If left unattended, the
branches wander and can become weakened and detached.
However, they respond well to proper guidance.

As a young branch on the Vine, you start out tender and
fragile but the Vine has inherent wisdom and knows what the
branches need. With your God-given unlimited potential for
growth, you need secure support so that you don't weaken and
break. You also need to be nourished and guided.

The Vinedresser provides rich well-cultivated soil and sup-
plies the basic nutrients. He also prunes away any dead wood
that prevents the production of good fruit. The art of pruning
requires a thorough knowledge of what each plant requires, how
it grows, and what is to be accomplished by pruning, so that
branches heal successfully. The Vinedresser knows just where to
cut so that each branch produces abundant fruit.

The Vinedresser will redirect your life, guiding you in ways
that are good for your soul. Once you make the choice to live
close to the Vine, you live with greater awareness of purpose.
Your priorities change and your new life may be incompatible
with your old ways. (Eph 4:20–24)

Even though you are attached to a Vine of superior stock,
there is much that you yourself can do to insure abundant fruit.

You can surround yourself with others who share your love and affinity for Jesus. You can protect yourself from spiritual disease by avoiding all that is not of God. Allow Jesus to nurture you with the truth of his Word. Let his living waters satisfy your thirst. Continually return to the Source of new life for renewal.

Have you noticed greater spiritual strength as you worked through the exercises in this book? Have you grown closer to God? Have you begun to experience inner healing. Do you feel more calm and peaceful? You may have noticed some physical improvement. Have minor physical symptoms such as headaches become less frequent? Are you sleeping more peacefully? These are symptoms of inner healing.

HELP WANTED IN THE VINEYARD!
DEDICATION REQUIRED

Because the healing ministry makes special demands on your energy, it is helpful to take a personal inventory before you begin. Is your spiritual life strong and solid? Are you overburdened with responsibilities? Do you need to realign your priorities? Take stock of your current emotional state. Are there volatile issues which need attention? Is your life in balance? Are you swamped with personal needs that require healing or resolution?

You are making a serious commitment. Can your family withstand the interruptions that accompany ministry? You cannot always schedule the Lord's work. A call for help may come at dinnertime, or just when you have settled down to watch a good movie with the family. Will loved ones support the additional demands on your time and energy? Do you have the stamina and flexibility to make yourself available to a larger family, God's family? Be honest with yourself.

Are you drawn to help others because God is calling you? Be sure that this is his desire for you, not yours. How can you be certain? Spend time in prayer asking for guidance, and then spend time in silence, listening. Discuss this ministry with your pastor, with your spiritual director, or with a wise friend whose judgement you trust. Sometimes when we think God is silent, he is speaking to us through others, perhaps through the very voices we ignore.

When you are in ministry, your own prayer life needs careful attention. You cannot continually dip into the well unless you replenish those waters from the Source. Learn from Jesus who prayed often. He modeled for us, through the example of servant leadership, the right way to minister. In ordinary leadership, the leader is the one in charge who makes all of the decisions. Jesus reversed this concept.

> ...anyone who wants to be great among you must be your servant, and anyone who wants to be first among you must be your slave, just as the Son of Man came not to be served but to serve, and to give his life as a ransom for many.
>
> (Mt 20:26–28)

Jesus washed the feet of his disciples. He went out among the crowds where he was most needed. Unlike a king on his throne holding court with the wealthy, Jesus was accessible to the needy people. He was available so that they could speak to him. They could come to him with their problems. In return, Jesus touched them with forgiveness and healing. He felt compassion for their suffering.

Jesus commissioned others to work with him so that he could teach more people about the Father's love. Initially, he chose the twelve apostles. Then, he enlisted the help of seventy-two others, saying,

> The harvest is rich but the labourers are few, so ask the Lord of the harvest to send labourers to his harvest. (Lk 10:2)

ARE YOU WILLING TO LABOR IN THE VINEYARD?

The call of Jesus for workers in the vineyard is a call for commitment. Jesus summons you, asking you to relinquish all that prevents you from serving him wholeheartedly. (Lk 14:33) Your reply requires careful consideration. When I said "Yes" to the ministry of healing, I had no idea of the impact this would make on my life. Your "Yes" to the Lord is a promise to follow through.

It represents a willingness to be used by him in whatever way he wishes, and not necessarily in the way you expect to be used.

You are probably anxious to begin. You need not wait for all of your physical ills to be cured, for your emotional troubles to vanish, and for your spiritual life to approach perfection. God will use you just as you are. However, it does help to be grounded in your own life before you invite the burdens of others. This ministry is emotionally and physically demanding.

When the woman tugged at Jesus' hem, he felt power go out of him. The ministry of healing can leave you feeling drained and depleted. You may find it difficult to sleep at night after you have poured out your heart in prayer. Jesus and his disciples went away for rest after teaching and healing. The more involved you become in ministry, the more you need to maintain a healthy balance in your own life.

Ministry requires that you do more than ever before, within the same twenty-four hours each day. Meanwhile, your primary responsibilities to your loved ones will not diminish. You need to take good care of yourself in order to meet the additional demands on your energy. You also must learn when and how to say no. One of the best ways to avoid burnout in ministry is to recognize your own limitations. Jesus does not expect you to minister singlehandedly to the entire world.

While ministry is tiring, it is also exhilarating to be a member of God's team. No matter how much you give of yourself to his little ones, you always receive more than you have given. You develop a deep reverence and love for the person who shares personal pain with you. Your lives become spiritually linked. No matter how objective you try to be, your heart will be captured by each person in pain.

YOUR THORN IS A CROSS TO EMBRACE

When you work for Jesus, the rewards far exceed the demands. The ultimate prize is his promise that we will be with him in paradise. However, the Jesus Walk has a price as well as a prize, and the price is substantial. Jesus promised to care for us, to protect us, and to provide for our needs, but he also promised the cross.

> Anyone who does not take his cross and follow in my footsteps is not worthy of me. Anyone who finds his life will lose it; anyone who loses his life for my sake will find it.
>
> (Mt 10:38–39)

In your initial excitement about your ministry, you feel elated. Your enthusiasm makes it difficult to imagine the prospect of any pain along the way. Starting ministry is like moving into a brand new house. You have a fresh start in life. You love the neighborhood. You look forward to meeting new friends. Everything about the house is clean and unsullied, waiting for you to imprint it with the stamp of your personality. What could possibly go wrong?

Once the newness wears off of your new surroundings, you realize that your old problems made the move with you. Your old personal baggage does not vanish when you begin ministry to others. You may have to struggle as St. Paul did with his "thorn in the flesh." (2 Cor 12–7) A thorn is a cross to embrace, a gift to keep you humble. Don't let the spectre of the cross discourage you from accepting the call to ministry. Jesus who walked the path to Calvary ahead of you, walks with you in ministry. Stay focused on him.

GOD'S HIDDEN AGENDA

When God healed my cancer and gifted me with a healing ministry, I felt richly blessed. Within a vibrant prayer community, my gifts were lovingly nurtured and my spiritual growth amazed me. I was deeply in love with the Lord and that was all that mattered. More and more, I prayed during the Eucharist that Jesus would empty me of all that was in the world. I wanted only to serve him and my ministry grew.

Then, after a few years, my husband accepted a career advancement which resulted in our move to a beautiful but isolated mountain house in Northern California. With our children living independently, this dream house perched on the hillside in a beautiful redwood forest seemed too good to be true. Then suddenly, I felt as empty as a bucket.

Due to a season of severe rainfall, the access road to our remote home suddenly disappeared, sliding down the mountain along with a neighbor's house. Our own house was intact but we were cut off from the outside world, with a mile-long, muddy hike up the mountain to the highway. The rain fell, more than 100 inches in about as many days. This constant downpour and the crackling sound of tall redwoods toppling night and day, along with an oozing mountain that showed no signs of stabilizing, led to sleepless nights.

An unsatisfying job, along with a barrage of insoluble problems on the mountain, was making my husband ill. He decided to change jobs. We weathered an uncertain passage of time. Our family was far away, our financial future was uncertain, and we had the commitment to pay for a house that we could not sell without a road. Meanwhile, it is hardly surprising that my ministry dried up. People were not likely to find a path to my door for prayers, given the condition of the path.

Then one day, the realization hit me. Jesus had answered my prayers. He had emptied me of everything. Jesus had even taken away the ministry which I loved so dearly. This was a dark time for my soul. I returned often to that vacant place within me and began to fill it by reading Scripture and spiritual books. It was a prayerful but not a joyful time.

Jesus helped me to mature spiritually by stripping away nearly everything I cared about. We still had our loved ones and our health. However, in lifting us up so high and then allowing us to fall, he changed our lives forever.

With the world crumbling around me, my deepest sadness was the loss of my grip on ministry. Perhaps I had been gripping it too tightly. Jesus taught me that I was insignificant. As I embraced my cross in the months that followed, I learned that his grace truly was sufficient for me. That period of dryness was merely a sabbatical, a time of growth and renewal for the work ahead. Jesus was refocusing my gaze upon him.

When we are busy looking at Jesus rather than at ourselves, he looks out for us. I seldom pray about my own needs.

Frequently, while I am busy ministering to others, Jesus solves my problems for me. This does not mean we will be free of burdens. There will always be trials but we endure ordeals with greater ease when we give them to Jesus.

When we meditate on our Saviour's cross and ponder his agony, we want to relieve his pain. We long to wipe his brow and to give him a cool drink of water. Similarly, when we suffer, Jesus stands with us. He will comfort us if we let him. There is nothing we can suffer that he did not suffer. The cross weighs less with the Lord's help. He wants to journey with us and lighten our burden so that we can be joyful witnesses to his triumph over evil.

As you minister to others, with your own cross wearing a tender groove in your shoulder, you will continue to receive blessings and additional healing. Nothing is wasted. Every pain or hurt you experience can be used to help someone else.

THE VINEDRESSER IS GENEROUS

Special healing gifts accompany some healings. For instance, a person healed of cancer may have a special gift of praying for cancer healing. However, your ministry will often require you to pray about complex problems. A person with cancer may also suffer mental depression. A woman with heart disease may be grieving over the breakup of her marriage. Someone with back pain also may have lost a child. This complexity of problems is best met when ministers pray together in teams.

The distinctive gifts of various members on a prayer team work together to accomplish the Lord's healing. Jesus sent out his disciples to minister in pairs, and he further promised that when two or more prayed together in his name, he would be there with them. He assures us that when we agree together in prayer, he hears us.

It is natural to feel self-conscious when you first begin praying over people. Don't worry if your style of praying is different from that of others. Jesus wants you to use the personal gifts you have received and one of those gifts is your own unique personality. Simply pray with faith in Jesus and with confidence in his love. Pray with a sincere heart. You will find your own style of praying.

When you join your prayers with those of others, you see the wonderful variety of healing gifts the Spirit has bestowed. One person has a powerful gift of praying with scripture. Another has keen discernment and the ability to touch the root cause of a person's problem. Still another prays with the thunder of authority, calling upon Jesus to fulfill his promises and perform a miracle.

One person may have a quiet gift of gentleness that soothes and calms turbulent emotions. Within a prayer team, some may pray in tongues, a prayer that often removes blocks to healing. Don't let the mannerisms of others distract you from your prayer. Keep your eyes fixed upon Jesus, and your mind and heart attuned to the whispers of his Spirit.

Some people who receive prayer may swoon while others do not. Being "slain in the Spirit" is a restful state which predisposes a person to healing. However, it is the Holy Spirit who places people at rest, not the prayer minister. When I was healed of cancer, some people grew faint during prayers for healing. I felt nothing, except the love and peace that was ministered to me. Yet I received a miracle.

Some prayer ministers have great gifts, others have lesser gifts. Your ministry is not about results, it is about praying. Jesus is the One who heals. In the parable of the workers in the vineyard, those who came to work late and worked the least were paid the same as those who started at dawn. The landowner said to those who complained, "Why be envious because I am generous?" (Mt 20:15)

You have been called to a privileged ministry. People who open their hearts to you deserve your respect of their privacy and their confidences. It is essential that you honor these little ones as children of the Father. Because of the sensitive nature of this ministry, it helps to have spiritual direction from someone of deep faith and prayer.

Your spiritual director will listen to your confidences and will offer wise guidance when you need it. Such an advisor can help you grow spiritually. The ministry of healing can be a heady business, but God will keep you humble if you stay attuned to his direction. You are merely a conduit for the healing power of Jesus. Your task is to minister his love in a way that gives him honor and glory.

COME WITH OPEN HEARTS AND HANDS

Imagine trying to work in the vineyard with hands clutching useless possessions and a mind that is preoccupied with worries. Encumbrances drain your energy and inhibit you. You need to arrive for work empty-handed.

Read John 15:1–2. How does your life need pruning?

List your worldly attachments and grade them on a scale of one to ten. (One is least resistance to letting go, and ten is great reluctance.) What can you relinquish now? Are your hands and heart open and receptive?

Stand with your arms outstretched wide. Now raise them higher. This is the posture of the cross. How does it feel? You are open—totally vulnerable—in a posture of total surrender! Your uplifted arms hold nothing—give everything. This is submission! Maintain this posture and pray, noticing how much easier it is to breathe when your arms are held high and your chest is expanded. Experience the liberation of empty hands. Maintaining this position, pray. Ask Jesus to fill your emptiness with a special gift.

There is one thing you cannot leave behind when you work for Jesus. He has invited you to pick up your cross and follow him. Your cross stays with you wherever you go.

Meditation on the cross:
Mary, the mother of Jesus, stands at the foot of the cross, gazing up at her Son's broken and lifeless body. She weeps. As his mother, she feels his agony more keenly than any other witness could. As a parent, she wants to take away his pain. All she can do is pray and love. Now Christ's body is placed in his mother's arms. She bathes his face with her own tears, and wipes his wounds with the sleeve of her garment. Her heart is pierced with sorrow. She holds Jesus.

What can you learn from Mary at the foot of the cross? How do you want to comfort Jesus?

Some symbols of Jesus' crucifixion include: the crown of thorns, the nails, the hammer, the sword, the garment that wrapped Jesus' body, drops of blood, Mary's tears.

Draw an outline of a cross. On it, draw the symbol that helps you relate to your Saviour, Jesus. Choose the one symbol that makes his suffering most meaningful to you. Meditate and pray with this symbol pictured in your mind.

Ask Jesus to give you a symbol that describes your own cross. Symbols are simple but powerful pictures that tell a story. Now add to the cross the symbol or symbols that best describe your personal cross. (If you cannot draw, use words to describe your cross.) When you place your burdens on his cross, you unite your suffering with Jesus.

Meditation:

Embrace the cross. The healing waters of Jesus flow from it. Jesus is hidden in your personal cross. It is there you will discover your treasure.

10. See How Much He Loves You

*"...after a prayer he laid his hands on the man
and healed him."* (Acts 28:8)

*W*ith your cross intersecting the cross of Jesus and your suf-
ferings enmeshed with his, your heart becomes one with
his heart. Your eyes see through his eyes. The cross eradicates the
divisive barriers of economics, politics, race, and creed. You pray
for others with the love and compassion Christ feels for them.

When Jesus heals hurts and sickness, he is saying, "See how
much I love you. See how much I want to be a part of your life."
Jesus cured ten lepers but the one who returned with praise and
thanksgiving received the gift of salvation. Without a conversion
of the heart, healing is incomplete. Each person should emerge
from your prayers with a deeper love for Jesus.

Let us assume that you have been asked to lead prayers of
healing for Jane, while others on the prayer group team pray
with you. This is your first opportunity to practice your healing
ministry, and it is an ideal situation.

YOUR LISTENING HEART

Before you pray, you need to know what kind of healing
Jane wants. Jane is in a wheelchair and your natural inclination
might be to pray about physical crippling. However, many illnesses can immobilize a person. If you launch into prayer for
Jane without first discerning her needs, you might be praying
for crippled limbs when the problem is a weakened heart.

Encourage Jane to briefly tell you what needs healing and
listen with care to what she says, as well as to what she does not
say. If Jane is uncomfortable discussing her problem, your non-

threatening questions can help her express what she wants to tell you. Many people come to a healing service with feelings of nervousness, embarrassment, and fear. Your gentleness will help put Jane at ease.

If you need further clarification, you can reflect back to her what she has said. For instance, "Jane, are you saying that you want God to heal the effects of polio, which has crippled you since childhood?" Perhaps Jane concurs, but you sense there is still something more she hasn't told you. Jane may not yet be ready to deal with deeper areas of woundedness.

You are only trying to discern how to pray for Jane. Rather than ask a lot of probing questions, allow the Holy Spirit to inform and guide your prayer. If Jane volunteers that she has hurtful memories of childhood rejection, you can include in your prayer a simple request for Jesus to touch the child within her. Jesus has always been with her, loving her even when others rejected her.

Jane may have fears about the future. Perhaps her husband died recently and she worries about the lonely years ahead. Or she might have deep concerns about her elderly and ailing parents. She may feel her own inadequacy and helplessness in meeting their needs. Your prayer for Jane can bolster her faith in God's providence for his children. He who cares about the birds in the sky and the flowers in the fields will never abandon her.

OFFER PRAISE AND THANKSGIVING

It is appropriate to recognize God's majesty with praise and thanksgiving before you present your petitions. Many of the Psalms begin and end with adoration, praise, and thanksgiving. Once you become comfortable with the prayer of praise, it will flow naturally in your daily prayer. Praise and thanksgiving will be on your lips and in your heart as you go about your everyday business. Excerpts from the Psalms can be interwoven with your own words.

An example of this prayer would be: "Lord, we praise you and we thank you. Glory to your name, Jesus. Your love is everlasting. You hear our pleas and come to our rescue. For this we thank you with our whole hearts. Lord, your love is everlasting. We sing your praises and bless your name for ever. Praise you, Lord. Thank you, Jesus."

Jesus often used the "laying on of hands" when he prayed for healing. In many instances, people were healed the moment he touched them. Prayerful touch is comforting. Your appropriate touch says that you are reaching out in Christ's love, that you care, and that you want to help. God uses your human contact to facilitate his healing.

Since sensitivity is essential, you can explain what you are doing. "Now I am going to place my hand upon your head while I pray. Is that all right with you, Jane?" Or you can ask, "Do you mind if I place my hand on your shoulder while I pray?" My preference is to pray with my hand resting lightly on top of the person's head. I have never had anyone refuse such a request.

Since healing should bring about a conversion of the heart, you can activate a person's faith by incorporating the suggestion in your prayer. An example of this would be: "Lord, we thank you for Jane's deep faith in coming to you tonight for healing…" By affirming Jane's faith, you help her recognize and experience her faith in an authentic way.

PRAY WITH FAITH, EXPECTATION, AND DISCERNMENT

When you pray for Jane, pray with expectation. God is faithful to his promises. You can reinforce Jane's faith by praying, "Lord, we praise you and we thank you for your promise that where two or three are gathered in your name, you are in their midst. You said that all we need to do is ask in your name, and our prayer will be answered…"

You and Jane can trust in his word because his healing does not rely upon your abilities as a healer. God's healing power is neither restricted by your lack of experience in praying for healing, nor is it limited by your inadequate vocabulary in voicing prayers. Jesus heals because he is God.

While you pray, ask God for further enlightenment. The Holy Spirit may bring to your mind words or images that will guide your prayer. If you are unsure how an image applies to

Jane, you can ask her. "Jane, I have an image of a woman in a rocking chair. She is holding a small quilt. Does that mean anything to you?"

Jane may be worried about her mother, who has Alzheimer's Disease and carries a baby quilt with her wherever she goes. Or perhaps Jane is still grieving for her grandmother, with whom she had a special relationship. Jane may have unresolved grief for an infant she lost prematurely. Learn to trust the inspiration of the Holy Spirit. If Jane cannot relate the image to her life, continue with your prayer. This does not mean that you or the Holy Spirit are in error.

As you pray, Jesus uses your faith in him to augment his healing powers. He told us that no one can come to the Father except through him. When Jesus promised that he will do whatever we ask in his name (Jn 14:13–14), he was teaching us to invoke his name when we pray. Always conclude your prayer by acknowledging the power signified by his name: "I ask this in the name of Jesus. Amen."

While you were praying for Jane, others on the prayer team were supporting your prayers, either with silent prayer or with the prayer language known as tongues. Using the discernment they received, they may follow your prayer with spoken prayers of their own.

If, after the team has prayed for Jane, she still seems to require more prayer, you might inquire, "Jane, is there something else we need to pray about?" or "I have a sense, Jane, that there is something you want to tell us so that we can pray more effectively."

You may have discerned that Jane needs to forgive someone. If you are receiving a strong impression from the Holy Spirit about this, you can pray on the strength of your discernment, even if Jane does not verbalize the problem. "Lord, I ask you to bring about the forgiveness Jane needs in her life. Help her to let go of any hurt feelings. Help her to forgive with the power of your love."

Perhaps Jane is harboring guilt about something she did or did not do, something that alienates her from the grace of God. She may feel uncomfortable about disclosing this, but you can pray, "Lord, I sense a spirit of guilt that is interfering in Jane's life. Since you know all things, Jesus, touch this problem and forgive Jane. Help her to receive your forgiveness, Lord, and to forgive herself for anything she may have done which separates her from your love and grace."

Some people have many layers of problems and you may touch on only one or two areas. The healing Jane receives today can lead to further healing tomorrow. If Jane's faith in God is deepened through your prayers, this is the best of all possible healings. She will be open to a more intimate relationship with Jesus and to future healing of her life.

At the conclusion of your prayer for healing, you may anoint Jane on the forehead with blessed oil. "I bless you, Jane, in the name of the Father, and of the Son, and of the Holy Spirit." You might feel led to anoint her hands to work for Jesus, and her feet to carry her on the path directed by Jesus.[24] The use of blessed oil was encouraged in the early days of Christianity. (Jas 5:14–16)

THE ABIDING PRESENCE OF THE HOLY SPIRIT

You may have noticed a sensation of heat in your hands while you prayed. Even if you were unaware of it, Jane may comment later that she felt heat or energy from your hands coursing through her body. This is the power of the Holy Spirit. Christ's Spirit is always present when we invoke it, even if is not felt. Manifestations often seem to occur in proportion to the praise offered by the people praying.

Other manifestations of the Spirit include an aroma of roses, of perfume, or of floral bouquets. Sometimes people who receive prayer are "slain in the Spirit." While slaying in the Spirit is a relaxed state conducive to healing, it is not a requisite for healing. This first happened to me at a large healing conference, a year after my cancer healing.

While I awaited prayers by Francis MacNutt, I locked one arm with my husband's arm, tightly gripping my purse in that hand. I was determined not to join the people on the floor all around us but God's sense of humor prevailed.

When the healer placed his hand upon my head and began to pray, my knees buckled and I fell backward, awkwardly extricating my entangled arm as I sank to the floor. An usher behind me steadied my fall but by the time I reached the floor, my wig had slipped forward and covered my eyes. The usher alternated between shouts of "Praise the Lord!" and fits of hysterical laughter.

Apprehensive people resist the Spirit's touch as I did, while others collapse immediately, sometimes before the prayer has been completed. One or two strong people can stand behind each prayer recipient and gently lower to the floor those who are overcome by the Spirit. Other prayer ministers continue to pray quietly over those resting in the Spirit while the healing service continues.

The faith of people you pray for is an important element in your healing prayers. Ideally, you both pray with faith that Jesus will hear and answer your prayers. While their faith in God may prompt people to ask for healing, Jesus also grants healings to deepen a person's faith. He may heal in order to draw closer to one who does not know him or to build faith in a person's medical team.

While the Lord has his own reasons for answering prayers for healing, Jesus repeatedly stressed the importance of faith. Two blind men who approached Jesus said they believed he could heal them. Their eyesight was restored when he touched their eyes saying, "Your faith deserves it, so let this be done for you." (Mt 9:29)

One woman had such deep faith in the power of Jesus to heal, she was instantly cured of a twelve-year hemorrhage by simply touching the fringe of his cloak. Jesus told her, "My daughter, your faith has restored you to health; go in peace and be free from your complaint." (Mk 5:34) He not only cured her, Jesus relieved any anxiety that her suffering would return. She was blessed with peace.

Jesus rewards faithful believers. A man named Jairus tried to approach Jesus because his twelve-year-old daughter was dying. When Jesus heard this, he said to the man, "Do not be afraid; only have faith." (Mk 5:36) Even though the child was dead by the time they reached the man's house, Jesus went to her bedside and told her to arise.

Jesus will reward your faith, too. You will pray with greater confidence as you grow in your ministry and observe the hand of God at work in the lives of those you serve. Continue to ask the Holy Spirit to increase your gifts and learn to trust the inspiration which comes from the Spirit.

USING ALL OF THE GIFTS

While the gift of discernment tells you how to pray for each person, the word of knowledge is a deeper insight into a person's prayer needs. It comes as flashes of insight or intuition, in mental images or words. However it appears, it arises in your mind with a strong certainty.

Once when praying over a young woman, all I saw was the color red and congested highways. To me these images represented anger and chaos but when I asked how the images related to her life, she saw no connection. The next day, however, she sought me out. When she had mentioned the images to her husband, he knew their meaning.

Her husband had been upset about the way her career changes were affecting their marriage. Even though he had been trying to tell her, she didn't seem to hear him. Our prayers, and the discernment of the Holy Spirit, resulted in improved communication between the couple. Their ensuing dialogue eventually restored harmony to their marriage.

The gift of tongues is usually one of the first given. If you don't have it, you can ask your prayer team to pray with you for the gift. By using the gift of tongues, you allow the Spirit to pray through you. It is an immense help, especially when you do not know how to pray. All of these gifts strengthen your prayer ministry.

Don't be discouraged if some people you pray for are not healed. Some illnesses require more than a brief prayer. Those who experience improvement but not a complete cure may need ongoing prayer for a total healing. Encourage those you pray with to continue praying for themselves, and remember them daily in your own prayers.

Ask those you pray for to let you know the results of your prayers. Their healing gives glory to God. In my prayer journal, I enter the names of those for whom I pray, along with the date and a brief description of each one's problem. I draw a large star next to each entry when the prayer is answered. My star-laden journal is a constant reminder of God's faithfulness to his promises.

THE IMPORTANCE OF NURTURING A HEALING

A person seeking healing through prayer should be encouraged to join a group where believers pray together. The spiritual conversion Jesus wants requires the kind of nurturing that is available in a spirit-filled group. It is also imperative that medical treatment ordered by the doctor is continued. When Jesus heals, the doctor will confirm the healing, just as the priest confirmed the healing of the lepers. There is grave danger in abandoning proper medical care against the doctor's advice.

It is important to listen to the counsel of the Holy Spirit when you pray, but keen discernment is essential. One woman ignored sound medical advice because her misguided adult children, claiming knowledge from the Holy Spirit that Jesus had already healed her invasive cancer, persuaded her to forgo the prescribed chemotherapy treatments.

When I learned about this, I tried to convince the woman that Jesus often works through doctors, who are qualified to recognize when the cancer is cured. However, she waited until her disease was in the final stages before submitting to the treatments. By then it was too late. The Holy Spirit was speaking to this mother through her doctor and through me, but she did not recognize his voice.

As you minister with prayers of healing, you will discover whether you have a large gift of healing or a small one. A few people are used by the Lord in a much greater way than others, but everyone can pray for healing. While you may never be famous for your healing ministry, you can be certain that Jesus will use your ministry to touch lives. Your prayers will be heard and lovingly answered.

The healing ministry has significance within your own family, as well as in the community. Family discord has existed since Adam and Eve. There are numerous theories about dysfunctional families, but no one has solved the problem. Prayer is the one remedy guaranteed to help.

You can be a prayer warrior for your loved ones, who will certainly benefit from your prayers. No matter how much we pray, we may not be the ones who will directly bring about the healing of our loved ones. Tomorrow, someone else may harvest the seeds of prayer that we plant today.

Some that you pray for will be physically healed, others will not. Some who are healed will be on fire with love of the Lord. Others who receive healing may not believe it is genuine. It isn't necessary for you to understand how God is working in the lives of others. There may or may not be miracles when you pray. This is all part of God's mystery and we are unable to explain it.

Jesus performed many miracles. Yet, in his home town of Nazareth, his healing power was rejected and ridiculed. Scripture says "...he could work no miracle there, though he cured a few sick people by laying his hands on them. He was amazed at their lack of faith." (Mk 6:5–6)

When you are the listening heart and the healing hands of Jesus, you will be loved by some and rejected by others. The only opinion that matters is that of the One you serve.

† † †

JESUS PRAYS WITH YOU

When Jesus calls you to ministry, he asks you to do things you never thought possible. Whenever you are in doubt about what to do, turn to Jesus and ask him. He will continue to teach and guide you through his Holy Spirit.

Meditation:

Imagine this scene. You have spent a long day sitting and listening to Jesus preach to the crowd on a hillside. He has attracted many people who crowd around him for healing. Now Jesus invites you to step into the crowd and pray for their needs. Immediately, a woman holds out her feverish baby to you. What is your response?

The crowd continues to press in around you and there are many who are sick. How will you handle this situation? Perhaps you can ask the people to join hands in a circle with you. As you all pray together for healing, you briefly anoint each person in the circle. Jesus does the rest.

Now imagine yourself walking with Jesus. He has taught you how to pray for healing and now you journey with him. As you enter a small village, ten lepers call out for mercy and healing. What is your reaction? Do you recoil from their open sores and their shabby clothing? Jesus goes toward them and speaks with them. Where are you in this picture? Do you rummage in your bag for rubber gloves and a face mask, or for a bottle of antiseptic? Jesus turns and looks at you. What does Jesus say?

Face your doubts and concerns honestly. Jesus understands human nature. Even though his work is challenging, he will give you all that you need to accomplish it.

Read Luke 10:1–20. What will you carry with you? What do you most fear as you go forth to minister?

When you turn your life over to Jesus, you can expect rejection from those who do not understand. Try not to take it personally. They may be at a different place on their journey with the Lord. Forgive, forgive and forgive again.

Imagine Jesus standing among friends and relatives in his home town. He is here to preach his Father's word, to cure people's sicknesses, and to work miracles. The very people who know him best turn away from him. They have no faith. Only a few are cured when he touches them. Jesus continues his journey and works some of his greatest miracles. The crowning miracle is his resurrection from the dead. What do you want to tell the people of Nazareth?

Read John 1:9–10. Do others see his light in you?

Meditation:

Imagine a world without light. There are no lightning bolts in the night sky, no dancing sparks in a fire, no magical dewdrops reflecting sunbeams. There is only darkness. Now see yourself as a light-bearer. You carry Jesus into the dark and broken places of the world. Light is the antidote to darkness.

> It is the same God that said, "Let there be light shining out of darkness," who has shone in our minds to radiate the light of the knowledge of God's glory, the glory on the face of Christ. (2 Cor 4:6)

11. The Light of Christ Overcomes Darkness

..."I am the light of the world;..." (Jn 8:12)

*W*e are summoned out of darkness into the light, called to walk as children of the light. St. Paul tells us that when we stay close to the Light, we reflect that Light to others. Light is warm and comforting. It dispels shadows, casts out fears, and beckons us to approach it. When we draw close to the flame, our shadows fall behind us and we feel secure.

Divine Light is the quality we share when we pray for inner healing. Just as there are different kinds of darkness, there are varying degrees and causes. Jesus brings hope. He repeatedly tells us not to be afraid because he is the Light who overcomes the darkness.

Regardless of the cause, people in darkness benefit from prayer. Problems of darkness range from those with temporary depression to those with serious psychological disabilities. Sandwiched in-between are people with less serious disorders that nevertheless prevent them from living life to the fullest. These include problems of anxiety, compulsions, obsessions, and phobias. Other categories of darkness include addictions as well as eating disorders and other unhealthy behaviors.

People whose lives are controlled by deviant behavior are buried in pockets of darkness. Even though professional treatment is indicated for many of these problems, spiritual companionship makes a positive difference. One of the challenges you face in praying for inner healing is understanding the nature of each person's problems.

BE GUIDED BY THE WISDOM OF THE HOLY SPIRIT

Ask your prayer group or other Spirit-filled Christians to pray with you for discernment, which is essential for ministering inner healing. The Holy Spirit tells you how to pray as well as when not to pray.

If you are not the one to bring Christ's healing to a person, you can simply pray for God's peace and provide a referral to someone whose gifts better match the need for healing. Even those who require professional help need to know that they are lovable, that they have value. The world may not understand, but Jesus does.

Any serious loss can cause a depressed state of mind. Support groups and counseling often help people recover more quickly from this temporary type of depression. Your prayer for the grief-stricken helps them walk into the light. Once they release loved ones to Jesus, they are better able to move through the necessary stages of grief recovery.

One type of depression, Seasonal Affective Disorder, is related to the changing seasons. Depression that is caused by the lack of sunlight during the shortened days of winter is relieved by exposure to light. Just as a lack of light can bring about depressive moods, an absence of Christ's light leaves people in the dark. Spiritual darkness is the most desperate kind but it is the desire of God's heart to shine within every person's soul.

People trapped in sinful ways cannot see the Light because they have placed a barrier between themselves and Jesus. This self-inflicted darkness results from a rejection of God, by knowingly and willingly committing a serious wrongful act. Serious sin is one of the contributing factors you must consider when you are pray for healing. Sinners have lost their way but you have the opportunity to lead people into the saving light of Jesus.

If, as a lay minister, you are praying with a person who is in a serious state of sin, your referral to a priest or minister is appropriate. Confession is redemptive and removes obstacles that otherwise block healing. (1 Jn 1:9) Jesus came to set the captives free and to release us from prisons of darkness. You help people choose life instead of darkness.

Inner healing strives to heal the effects of traumatic events, hurtful words, and damaging actions that have left invisible marks on the inner person. From an objective viewpoint, the healing minister helps a person look inward to locate and examine those painful memories.

Healing of deep interior regions involves more than prayer. It requires a willingness on the part of the wounded person to make contact with the pain and to forgive those who caused it. Without reconciliation and transformation, the pain of inner hurts remains.

Serious disorders call for serious measures, including drug treatments, counseling, or long-term therapy. Mental health professionals have special training and skills that enable them to help the mentally ill. As a minister of healing, you share the professional's goal of helping the person with emotional pain, but your approach is different.

HOW JESUS USES YOU TO BRING ABOUT HEALING

It is important to recognize your limitations. You need to be aware of what you may and may not do. As a prayer minister, you wouldn't attempt to operate on a fractured hip. Neither should you consider yourself qualified to heal a fractured life. What you may do for the person with deep emotional wounds is provide loving support and prayer.

You can prop up people with God's love as they journey toward wholeness. With the Holy Spirit, you may even walk part of the healing journey with them. Deep inner healing requires the recall of forgotten memories. Through prayer, the shadowy corners of the troubled soul are illuminated and transformed by the light of Christ.

Inner healing is proportional to the willingness of a person to forgive. When Peter asked how many times he must forgive someone who wronged him, Jesus answered seventy times seven. Seven was considered a holy number and seventy times seven conveyed the idea of infinity.[25] Jesus was saying, "You must forgive endlessly." This is especially true in healing relationships and buried hurts.

The inner healing process has been compared to the peeling of an onion but there is far more to healing than this. Once old layers of hurts are uncovered, each memory may require forgiveness. Healing prayer sometimes succeeds where psychotherapy has failed, because prayer can bring closure to old wounds.

As the leader of a small group that met weekly to discuss parish renewal, I had difficulty keeping the group focused. Discussions about family problems continually disrupted and blocked the progress of our renewal program. One evening, I decided to open the meeting with a short meditation. It was my hope that people would then be able to set aside their problems and concentrate on the purpose of the meeting.

Each member of the group was invited to relax and visualize someone they needed to forgive, a person who aroused their feelings of resentment. Each was given an opportunity to mentally vent feelings of anger and then to see the situation from the other's viewpoint. Finally, they alternated between images of Jesus on the Cross and themselves with the person they needed to forgive. This continued until they received reconciliation and forgiveness with that person at the foot of the cross.[26]

Once resentments are released, people are able to approach the cross, arm in arm with the ones they have forgiven. To my surprise, however, a number of healings resulted from that one meditation. One person became less fearful. Communication improved between the married couples, a troubled family moved toward reconciliation, and our meetings became more productive.

The most dramatic healing occurred in a man with a stuttering problem. During his meditation, he was surprised to see the face of a teacher who had humiliated him in the first grade. Recognizing the root cause of his speech problem, he was moved by the Cross to forgiveness. Later, after further prayers for healing, he overcame his impediment.

Speech is a gift given only to the human species. How ironic that this gift of words, which enables us to sing praises to God and to make the world a happier place through our encouragement and affirmation, can also turn us against one another.

Our words have the power to destroy the morale of others, both in and outside of the family.

> The tongue that soothes is a tree of life;
> the barbed tongue, a breaker of hearts. (Prv 15:4)

In the healing ministry, Jesus uses your mouth to speak his words of comfort when you pray. You can consecrate your gift of speech to ensure that your words sing, rather than sting. Ask Jesus to put a guard over your lips. Ask him to bless your speech, and to speak through you the words he wants others to hear. Learn to pray before you speak, especially in difficult situations. Christian diplomacy enables you to enjoy relationships that are blessed, not broken.

THE KEY THAT OPENS DUNGEON DOORS

Forgiveness is a key element in inner healing because it removes hidden barriers. Many who come for healing are unaware that they have a deep need to forgive. In order for the light of Christ to penetrate their dark dungeons of resentment, they need to own and release the old hurts and angers that prevent them from loving.

We learn and grow when we honestly acknowledge our failings and make reparation. Just as you forgive another, you can forgive yourself. Everything you do to achieve healing in your own life and relationships will be helpful to your healing ministry.

During confession at a contemplative retreat, I described the ongoing difficulty I encountered with a person whose bitterness brought constant tension into our relationship. The wise priest who listened advised me to surround this difficult person with love and prayer every day. My penance was threefold. I must have repentance for my own sinfulness in this relationship, I must ask God to release this person from depression and negativity, and I must hold that person in light and love.

As I prayed and contemplated the priest's advice, the Lord instructed me further. He explained that my constant complaints about the person's bitterness sowed more seeds of bitterness. I was actually perpetuating bitterness with my disparaging thoughts and words. As a result, I reaped the bitterness that I had sown.

In order to heal the relationship, Jesus told me to let go of my own bitter feelings and sow love. I thanked Jesus for removing my blinders and I asked him for the special grace I needed to make this difficult change. Through prayer and forgiveness, the relationship improved my attitude and my behavior changed.

Inner healing always involves change. We all find it more than just difficult to change ourselves but once we recognize the need to change, we must be willing to change. Through determination to make it happen and patience with the process, the change will occur. With the help of God's grace, we can change ourselves but we cannot change another.

Jesus said that the faults we see in another are nothing compared to our own large faults, to which we are blind. (Mt 7:3–5) While you cannot change another, you should be alert to those traits that you find intolerable in others. What is it about another that "drives you up the wall"? You probably harbor similar traits within yourself. The dark shadowy aspects which we hide from ourselves are the very ones we react to and loudly criticize in others.

JESUS FREES HIDDEN MEMORIES

Some people experience a deep and inexplicable sadness. Others may feel the eruption of a sudden mood of loneliness when it is least expected. Symptoms of buried hurts can include: sudden outbursts of anger; inexplicable feelings of abandonment and rejection; perceptions of being unloved or unworthy of love; and feelings of shame.

In an adult, the hurt associated with hidden memories can induce phantom waves of melancholy and sadness. Something as innocent as a word, a facial expression, a tone of voice, a dream, a scene in a movie, or music on the radio can mysteriously trigger strong emotions associated with a forgotten painful memory.

Even when a memory from the past has been touched, it may seem vague and elusive. With or without a connection between memories and feelings, intense emotions can evoke moods of uneasiness, fear, depression, hostility, and anxiety.

There are numerous causes for inner wounding and so many ways that hurts from the past can affect the present. The unborn fetus shares a lifeline with the mother through its connection to the placenta. In addition to nourishment, it receives the effects of any chemicals ingested by the mother. If the mother abuses her own body with drugs, cigarettes, alcohol, or caffeine, the fetus is affected.

It is thought that the unborn child also shares in the mother's emotions. A pregnant woman may be happy or sad, healthy or ill, she may feel loved or unloved. The unborn child participates in the mother's emotional highs and lows.

When I was present at the birth of a grandson, I saw the miraculous birthing process, with its drama and tension, from an entirely new perspective. Traditionally, we give our sympathy to the mother, who can articulate the discomfort and weariness of childbirth. The emerging infant, however, arrives from the strenuous and laborious ordeal unable to express its feelings of pain and fear. Dislodged from its safe refuge within the mother, the newborn is plunged into a foreign environment and must learn to communicate its needs.

While newborn infants require nourishment, it is also vital that they receive love. So much is communicated through touch, and a mother's normal touch is gentle and comforting. If the mother is overtired, ill, worried, or emotionally stressed, she may lack sufficient energy to interact lovingly with her child. There might be an absence of the special language of cooing between parent and baby. Also, the infant feels tenseness in the mother's body and senses strain and irritation in her voice.

Tiny human creatures record both positive and negative perceptions. Even though many early emotional experiences are forgotten by the conscious mind, they can leave an imprint. As the infant becomes a toddler, new memories overlay earlier ones. Memories of love and affirmation are stored along with those of spankings and harsh words.

Even the child who feels secure as an infant can have negative experiences during the early school years. Nursery school or kindergarten introduces a complexity of challenges to the free spirits of children, who now must conform to a structured environment. Even trips to the bathroom are regulated by bells and schedules.

In the mind of a child, teachers may seem unfair and the taunting of schoolmates can feel cruel. Children who enter school with self-esteem intact can become insecure. They may feel discouraged by the need to compete with peers, as they see themselves judged and graded on everything they do. Home life changes too, with the imposition of homework and with strong parental pressures to succeed.

Thus far, we have only considered the child in a normal environment. This does not take into account the special problems of children who are traumatized by physical or sexual abuse, or whose families are crippled by alcoholism, drug abuse, poverty, separation, and other problems. As the child matures, each stage of growth brings new problems. Many of these result from peer pressures to conform.

Through the fault of no one, a child can become traumatized at any age. Children who don't understand the sudden absence of a parent often blame themselves. Childish thoughts include: "If I hadn't yelled at Mommy, she wouldn't have gotten sick." Or, "It's all my fault that Daddy died, because I got mad and wished he was dead!"

Children in troubled circumstances sometimes reach irrational conclusions. Impressions of being unloved, abandoned, or guilty are falsehoods because each one of us has been loved by God from the instant of our creation. Even during those times when we felt deserted or rejected, Jesus did not abandon us. Similarly, self-blame for the problems of others results in neurotic guilt. Children are not responsible for the shortcomings of their parents.

JESUS, THE LIGHT OF TRUTH WHO SETS US FREE

When the child's mistaken perceptions are carried into adulthood, they become erroneous opinions that masquerade as the truth. Jesus came into the world as the Word of Truth spoken by the Father. The truth of his love for you is the light which exposes and corrects falsehoods. Only when error is brought into the light of truth can it be corrected, for truth sets us free. (Jn 8:31–32)

When the inner child's hurts are uncovered and touched by Jesus, the adult is transformed. Jesus, who was with the child through the difficulties, redeems the past and carries that child into emotionally healthy adulthood. The person feels lovable and begins to see perpetrators of the hurts through the eyes of Jesus. Forgiveness makes the healing complete. Even though the once-painful memories still exist, the pain is replaced by the love and peace of Jesus.

In ministry, you can be a good sounding board. The sound board in a string instrument reinforces tones by means of sympathetic vibration. When you allow people to bounce their thoughts against you, they often find that they can work through their own problems.

In praying with a person for inner healing, there are several ways that you can help. First of all, you can be present to the pain. While you cannot resolve another's problems, you can provide the comfort of companionship on the healing journey.

Often the best gifts you can offer another person are your quiet attention and interest. In a one-on-one healing situation, the person with inner hurts has special needs for prayer. When you listen, do so with your eyes, your ears, and your body. People are uncomfortable about confiding to a disinterested listener. Remember, you are presenting the face of Christ to one of his little ones.

Attentive listening gives you the knowledge required to help your prayer. Keep an open mind because your role in healing involves prayer, not judgement. Ask the Holy Spirit to speak his guidance to you. Don't be too quick to suggest a solution for every problem. The healing process takes time. When you allow people opportunities to make their own discoveries, they may achieve inner healing more quickly.

As you listen without judging, the message you send says "You are loved. You have value. Your story is important." This kind of validation is not only healing, it often helps a person to solve a problem.

As you listen with the heart and mind of Jesus, each person you pray for will begin to build a bridge between deeply buried hurts and troubling feelings. This is what happens when we allow God, who shines in our minds, to radiate the minds of others with the light of God's glory.

ILLUMINATION BRINGS TRANSFORMATION

The world is filled with shadows but you need not fear them. Shadows are merely an indication that a bright light is shining nearby. Jesus invites you to bring his healing light into the dark recesses of the soul. He will illuminate the darkness and heal the brokenness there.

Label one column "Life Giving" and the other "Broken." List your relationships accordingly. How can you nurture the relationships in Column One? How can you repair those in Column Two?

Through the healing of memories and emotions, Jesus repairs interior damage caused by painful memories and replaces them with his love. This inner healing requires cooperation. In order to become a new creation, a person must be willing to enter the old wounds and probe the emotions that accompany the memories.

A Story:

Imagine yourself a lowly little caterpillar. You cannot travel far and you are unable to move quickly. You can only go where your stubby little legs carry you. You spend a lot of time crawling in dirt. Worms and insects live in your neighborhood. This travel makes you hungry, causing your stomach to growl. Attracted by a tree with an abundance of green, life-giving leaves, you climb high.

You munch away happily, stuffing yourself with good food. The long hard climb and all that chewing makes you sleepy. It would be wonderful to curl up and take a nap. You spin a little nest for yourself on a secure tree branch. Then you crawl inside your new home and sink into a long, comfortable slumber.

When you awaken, you feel different. You stretch and try to move around, but your little legs are gone. Instead, you now have two large flappy appendages that appear useless. You thrash around, trying to shake them off. In the process, the fabric of your nest is torn. Light streams in through the opening and a fresh breeze is blowing.

You wiggle and flap, trying to disengage yourself from your torn nest. Suddenly, you are free. You perch on the tree branch and begin to stretch again, but the breeze lifts your appendages and you are airborne. When you flap, you fly with grace and beauty. You can fly high and low. You can even make lovely figure-eights in the air. You admire your colorful wings and you don't even miss your stubby legs. Enjoying this freedom, you look down at the ground and wonder, why would anyone choose to live like a worm?

An Opportunity:

Learn to fly! Every morning, thank Jesus for all of your gifts, for your new positive attitude, and for the happy discoveries you will make about yourself today. Thank him often during the day and ask him to increase your awareness of the goodness in yourself, as well as in others. You will be amazed with the results, as Jesus transforms your dark, negative aspects into beams of his sunshine and light. Not only will you feel different, others will react positively to the change they see in you.

Give a compliment to God. Now give one to yourself.

12. Jesus Heals the Brokenhearted

"He has sent me to bring good news to the poor,
to bind up hearts that are broken;..."
(Is 61:1)

Even though we live in an "age of enlightenment," a great number of people are still stumbling in the dark, wondering who turned out the lights. Many of them are being led by an angry little child. Have you discovered your inner child? Did you find an angelic little darling or a spoiled brat? Mine is a little of each.

My little kid is seven years old, thinks she is really cute, loves to do creative things, and rushes in where angels wouldn't dare. Like most children her age, she often lacks the skill to be diplomatic. Instead, she just blurts out whatever comes to mind. My inner child is lovable to me because she is mine but the better I know her, the more I understand how she upsets other adults. Now that I recognize her voice, I am teaching her better manners.

A breakthrough in meeting my inner child occurred after I was directed to dialogue with her in writing. I was instructed to print with colored markers on large sheets of paper, using my less dominant hand when my inner child spoke.

Even though my scrawl was like that of a small child, the kid inside had a lot to say. When I began to really listen to this child, we became good friends. One of the first things she disclosed is that she wants a sandbox. While I haven't delivered on that promise, I have kept my word to spend more time playing so that she doesn't get cranky.

YOUR INNER CHILD HAS NEEDS TOO

There are some telltale signs that help you recognize your wounded inner child. Are you defensive when you receive constructive criticism? Do you overindulge in work, forgetting to take time to play? When you open your mouth to speak, do ugly toads pop out? If so, the child inside wants healing.

From the child within you can learn about your joys as well as your disappointments. You might rediscover what it is like to be a child. You may be chided to stop wasting time on boring stuff and to spend more of your energy on worthwhile activities, such as watching clouds, smelling flowers, and using your imagination. When your inner child feels you can be trusted, you might learn some long-kept secrets that will advance your inner healing. This child remembers things that you have forgotten.

Charles L. Whitfield, M.D., describes the child within as the part of us that is "ultimately alive, energetic, creative and fulfilled." That vibrant, creative child is the healthy inner child but he estimates that as many as 80 to 95% of us grew up without the love, nurturing, and guidance that we needed.[27] This hurt child drains your creative energy and contributes to relationship problems.

When someone else's hurt little inner child throws a poison dart at your own inner child, the relationship breaks down and a disagreement becomes a major conflict. Feelings are hurt, a line is drawn in the sand, and before anyone realizes what has happened, the childish controversy has escalated into all-out war. Relationship wars cause pain, and this is where inner healing can help.

There are so many ways people are wounded, and some hurts are like deep puncture wounds festering with poison. They have to heal from the inside out. God can heal something that happened way back in your childhood because he exists outside of time. You can invite Jesus to go into your past and, with his love, bring healing to old injuries. This is called the healing of memories.

You have already learned some ways that buried memories of childhood injuries unknowingly inflict pain in adulthood. The healing of deep emotional pain is challenging due to the subjective nature of the inner life. While physical pain can be described by its location and intensity and can be diagnosed through tests, deep inner healing is more complex.

Deep-seated inner pain is difficult to describe. A person suffering emotionally may not recognize the source of the pain because with many layers of hurts, the boundaries become blurred. Complex inner pain may be summed up by the simple statement, "I can't explain it. I just feel awful!"

THE ANCIENT PATH WITHIN

A striking analogy to the labor involved in inner healing can be drawn from the work of researchers in Tanzania, where archeologists have carefully uncovered and preserved the Laetoli Trail, a path of primitive footprints. "Each imprint is only a memory held in the earth of a creature that walked the plains long before the first modern humans were born."[28] Past hurts leave imprints on the unconscious mind comparable to the footprints left by ancient people walking that East African trail.

Even though the team that first discovered the fragile prints took the precaution of burying them under a protective layer of gravel, the trail was besieged by forces of nature. There was increasing danger that the clear outlines of the fragile prints would become obliterated, due to continuous erosion and the invasion of tree roots.

Healing the disappointments and hurts of life involves excavation of the trail of imprints, which are buried in the unconscious mind beneath layers of memories. The more painful the hurts, the more deeply they are buried until the memories become blurred or forgotten. As a person continues forward on life's journey, the hurts remain hidden until there is a serious recognition of the need for wholeness.

Recent restoration of the Laetoli Trail began with the clearing of boulders, rocks, and soil until the protective layer of gravel was reached. Then, wearing white gloves and working with brushes and wooden picks, the conservationists carefully removed fine particles of clay to expose the ancient footprints.

After analyzing and recording the prints, the team secured

the trail to prevent future erosion and root damage. Finally, the trail was covered with lava boulders and the village people were encouraged to dedicate their ancestral trail as a sacred site. Healing of past hurts requires a similar process of discovery and restoration to wholeness.

As you journey with a person to the ancient burial site of forgotten hurts, you listen with compassion to the unfolding story. Inner restoration begins by unearthing the forgotten hurts. As a companion on the journey inward, you help remove some of the boulders that obstruct the ancient trail. Beneath these boulders, additional layers may obscure the imprinted memories.

EXCAVATION IN PROGRESS! WHITE GLOVES REQUIRED!

The "white glove" stage of inner healing demands skill and sensitivity to uncover painful memories. This work is important because the memories are clues to long-forgotten feelings, sensations, and perceptions that the mind has recorded and stored.

Just as the ancient footprints were painstakingly uncovered and brought into the light, the minister of healing shines the light of Jesus on a person's buried hurts. For instance, an uncovered memory of abandonment might recall the devastation a child felt when left in the care of strangers. Jesus can go into the past and heal the frightened child, removing the pain of the memory.

Memories can be prayed about and healed as they are uncovered. The longer form of prayer for the "Healing of Memories" is more detailed. It begins with the moment of conception and any rejection or difficulties the unborn child might have experienced through the union of the parents. The healing prayers continue on through the *in utero* period, the moment of birth, and early childhood on into young adulthood.

Prayers about painful memories help the healing process as Christ's love brings newness. A reverence for the sacred site of the inner self ensures protection against future relapse for those healed. There can be no darkness in those who live as light-filled holy shrines.

After you have walked this difficult path with Jesus, you

may be called upon to help another person dislodge life's boulders. You may be the one who helps that person burrow through the layers concealing the source of inner pain. You may even share some little thing from your own experience that will help that person to have an "Aha!" experience. When your prayers result in Christ's inner healing, the transformation is wonderful to behold. As Isaiah prophesied, you are rebuilding ancient ruins. (Is 58:12)

While you cannot do another person's actual digging to the heart of the problem, you can carry the shovel and the tools. You may be able to point out the best place to dig, but digging is an individual matter. Much of this inner work can only be accomplished from within. Because this type of healing involves a growth process, it also requires perseverance.

The way that you pray for each person will vary, just as each person's needs will vary. Humans are a complex blend of mind, body, and spirit all working together. Whatever affects one area affects the others too.

HONORING AND CONSECRATING THE SACRED SITE

Remember Jane? One day, she calls. While she didn't experience the physical healing she had hoped for, she has noticed a slight physical improvement. Jane overcomes her timidity and asks for a favor. "You know, you prayed that Jesus would touch the child within me. Well, he has and I just wondered if I could see you again. I still don't feel right. Maybe I need some more healing."

In a private setting, Jane is now ready to tell you more about her life. She describes her childhood before the onset of polio. As you listen, observe her body language and the emotions in her voice. If her voice begins to quaver or if tears well up in her eyes, make mental note of the emotionally charged material she is disclosing. You can pray about these memories at the proper time.

You inquire about the ways that polio affected Jane's life. Ask her to describe what she felt. What else was going on in her life at that time? You are still building a healing relationship and this cannot be rushed.

When you are ready to pray about the new hurts Jane has uncovered, begin with praises to Jesus. Thank him for the love he showers upon his children. Thank him especially for always being present in Jane's life, and for touching the little child within her. Thank him for inviting her to draw closer to his healing light, and for his loving response to your prayers, as shown by her slight physical improvement.

Ask Jesus to continue the healing work he has begun in Jane. Pray about any fears or concerns that Jane has shared, and request further enlightenment by the Holy Spirit. Close your prayer by asking these blessings in the name of Jesus.

DEEP INNER HEALING IS A PROCESS

The intervals between healing sessions allow Jane to process what has happened. The Holy Spirit may use this time to bring more buried memories to Jane's awareness. The next time Jane is more relaxed and comfortable and she is prepared to delve a little deeper. Jane mentions that initially she felt great after you prayed with her, but lately she has felt very tired. She has not been sleeping well.

As Jane continues to share her story with you, you are led by the Spirit to probe more deeply. Since Jane has already shown shyness and reticence about examining her past, you will want to be sensitive. She may not yet be ready to tackle the deepest areas of emotional pain. Do not push Jane into areas she is unready to discuss.

You ask Jane to tell you more about her childhood. Your questions can encourage Jane to explore problems surrounding her polio. "How did you feel about yourself growing up?" or "Did your disability cause you special problems in school?" or "How did your family treat you when you were unable to keep up with your brothers and sisters?" While these are valid questions and the answers might lead to a deep inner healing, you allow Jane to set the pace.

Even though Jane is in a wheelchair, she may have great

self-esteem. It is possible that she received a lot of love from her family, excelled in school, had many friends, and was elected class president in high school. If all of these things are true, you can help Jane praise Jesus for the positive blessings in her life.

Your questions lead Jane to break new ground. She says "Everyone gave me a lot of love and recognition, but I was always ashamed of the way I walked. My family was loving but the kids at school ridiculed the braces on my legs. When they chose team members for games, no one wanted me."

Her disclosures about feeling rejected may lead to even deeper areas of pain. At some point, you discern that beneath a meek and quiet appearance, Jane has a lot of buried anger, perhaps even rage. In childhood, she may have thought that people would not like her if she vented her painful emotions. After years of keeping a lid on these emotions, she feels like a powder keg, ready to explode.

In the same way that some people postpone seeing a doctor until their symptoms are unbearable, Jane has postponed dealing with her anger until it is intolerable. You discern that Jane's anger is trying to erupt. This could be the reason for her recent fatigue and sleeplessness. The power of this emotion frightens her.

You decide not to probe further into Jane's childhood at this time because her disruptive emotions signal a greater need. Powerful emotions are charged with energy. They are emotionally draining. Part of the healing process requires that we learn how to channel our destructive emotions into useful and lifegiving energy. This is something Jane is ready to learn.

Reassure Jane that the ongoing prayers for healing are being heard, in spite of her fatigue and sleeplessness. Deep healing requires time, patience, and trust in Jesus as he walks with her through the pain of the past. Help Jane to understand that it isn't her fault that her healing is progressing slowly. Jesus intends a deeper healing.

The Holy Spirit is revealing unforeseen areas for healing. Affirm Jane's faith and her willingness to walk with Jesus into the regions he wants to heal. Pray with Jane about her disruptive emotional feelings. Thank the Holy Spirit for bringing these emotions to the surface for healing. In your prayer, reassure Jane that the feelings are not bad.

Ask Jesus to help Jane trust in his protection as she examines her emotions. Ask him to bless her with deep and peaceful sleep each night, and to minister to her while she slumbers. Include a petition for the healing of any new memories Jane has shared. Before she leaves, encourage Jane to meditate on St. Paul's encouraging words:

> The trials that you have to bear are no more than people normally have. You can trust God not to let you be tried beyond your strength, and with any trial he will give you a way out of it and the strength to bear it. (1 Cor 10:13)

Jesus is a gentle healer. He knows what each one needs in order to be whole. Jane's inner healing is occurring in stages. As the Holy Spirit continues to bring memories to the surface, Jane may be able to pray for her own healing. If she reaches a roadblock, she may ask for additional help.

> ...on those who live in a land of deep shadow
> a light has shone. (Is 9:1)

Through your prayers as a member of Christ's restoration team, the people you pray with experience sanctification of their inner hurts. You help them expose their ancient imprints to the healing light of Christ.

JESUS MAKES US FUNCTIONAL

Jesus loves little children and he loves the wounded child within you. He wants to help that child face the nightmares and skeletons of the past so that he can restore the child to health.

Meditation:
You step into a dark closet and close the door. You thought you would be alone but now you hear the frightening rattling of bones. You turn on your flashlight and discover that there are toothless old skeletons in the dark with you. Suddenly, they march out of the closet and continue right out the front door. Seen by daylight, they no longer frighten you. You realize that they are harmless.

Hidden secrets in a family have devastating effects. Brought out into the light, they lose their power. Dysfunction is a fancy name for the human condition in which we find ourselves. The bad news: we are dysfunctional people. The good news: Jesus makes us functional.

Read the Third Lamentation in the Book of Lamentations. It describes the sorrow, despair, and darkness felt by people who had turned away from God. The people examine the cause of their misery, admit their wrongs, repent, and pray for reconciliation. It contains elements of inner healing.

> …Yahweh is good to those who trust him,
> to the soul that searches for him." (Lam 3:25)

Read Psalm 139 whenever you feel you are coming unraveled. Thank God for the wonder of you.

An Activity:
Take your inner child on an outing. This little one wants to spend quality time with you. Go to visit the zoo, just the two of you. No other adults, please! This special day will help you to become better acquainted. A zoo is a wonderful place to stroll and to experience the sights and sounds around you.

Perhaps the zoo has a merry-go-round, or a miniature steam train. Take your inner child on a ride. Eat an ice cream cone. Throw peanuts to the animals if that is permitted. These are all kid things, and fun to do. The chimpanzees and the monkeys want to entertain you. Notice how they interact with one another as they play. Does the baby cling to its mother as she swings from place to place? Can you watch their antics without smiling and laughing?

Visit the nursery and notice how newborn animals are given warmth, security, and affection. They have special needs, just like human babies. When a newborn animal is rejected by its mother, another animal sometimes takes the mother's place, providing needed nourishment and nurturing.

If your childhood needs were not met, you can reparent your inner child. Begin by giving yourself a big hug!

13. Allowing God to Be God

"Pause a while and know that I am God...."
(Ps 46:10)

Sooner or later in your healing ministry, you will struggle to understand why some people that you pray for do not appear to be healed. The answer lies with God. Healing is his business. I believe that God always answers our prayers in the way that is most loving. He wants what is best for each one of us. We think we know what we need, but God who knows better answers our prayers with divine wisdom.

At times, Jesus may choose you as the spiritual companion who walks the entire journey with a person in need of healing. At other times, you may be only the one who sheds light on the path, but does not go the entire distance with a person. Others may be used by God to complete the work. God has his own reasons for healing, but one element is constant. Jesus brings people into deeper relationship with his Father.

HEALING IS GOD'S BUSINESS; PRAYING IS OURS

Sometimes we only see the problems before us. If we could peek around the corner and see the wonderful surprises God has in store for us, our view of current difficulties might change. Often, it is only when we look back on our lives that we understand where God was leading us during difficult times. I have finally learned to trust in God's goodness, no matter how bad things seem.

As you minister the healing of Jesus and discern how to pray, you will rule out obstacles that may exist within the person you pray for. Don't become discouraged if you do not see immediate results when you pray. Healing can be in progress even though it is not apparent. While you are praying for a physical healing, Jesus may be healing deep inner hurts.

The person receiving inner healing may not be aware of what God is doing within. Since inner healing is a process, the results may be recognized gradually. If you have suffered from a chronic muscle pain, you remember what an annoyance it was. Every time you moved a certain way, the pain was there. Then one day, you realized that the pain had vanished. Inner healing occurs in a similar way. One day, a new feeling is recognized where once there was pain.

TAKING DOWN THE WALL BRICK BY BRICK

One major obstacle to physical healing is the need for reconciliation on the spiritual level. If a person's relationship with God is not healthy, physical healing may be thwarted. Your prayers can help that person come to better terms with God. As you learn to deepen your own relationship with the Father, with Jesus, and with the Holy Spirit, you become more sensitive to this need in others. Every tiny seed of faith in another can be encouraged as you pray for healing.

The need for inner healing can be a major impediment to physical healing. Medical science has discovered many ways that emotions collaborate with the body to affect health. Your gentle questioning may uncover emotional wounds that will respond to prayer. While physical healing can be verified by the doctor, inner healing is more subjective. Sometimes an unknown burden is quietly removed by Jesus without fanfare.

Deep inner healing liberates those who suffer emotional distress caused by the words or actions of others. We have discussed some ways that the emotional pain of forgotten hurts can be transformed and understood in a new way. That is only a part of the metamorphosis Jesus desires. He wants hearts, minds, and souls set on fire with love for God.

Grudges, resentment, and bitterness are serious obstacles to healing. A person must be willing to break down the walls of negative attitudes so that grace and healing can freely flow. A refusal to forgive and resolve conflicts may be enmeshed with sinful attitudes, such as pride or envy. These sins are in direct opposition to love.

God is love, and sins against love include attitudes and actions of apathy or indifference toward God. It is not possible to look in two directions at the same time. You cannot look at God while you are looking away. Sinfulness can be a serious impediment to healing but renunciation of the sin and repentance remove this obstacle.

In addition to those who suffer hurts caused by others, there are many who bring suffering upon themselves through unwise choices. Even so, their choices may be influenced by hurts in the distant past. No wonder inner healing is so complex!

People often make bad choices in an attempt to relieve inner pain. Unhealthy relationships lead to the compromise of moral values. Drugs, alcohol, gambling, criminal activity, promiscuous behavior, and eating disorders bring only temporary relief while masking and compounding the pain. One way or another, God's wonderful creation becomes battered and bruised as layer by layer, new scar tissue overlays the old.

Not only are most addictions self-destructive, they also have serious social consequences. While everyone can benefit from prayer, people with addictions may need the additional intervention of professionals in the fields of medicine and psychology. You may discern that you should refer the person to another whose healing gifts are greater than yours. Addictions are just one area in which you may not be the one who will bring about God's healing.

For those suffering from serious mental disorders, such as schizophrenia, paranoia, and clinical depression, a normal life is not an option. Their illnesses set them apart from the rest of society. While you can pray for and encourage these afflicted people, they require professional diagnosis and proper treatment.

ATTITUDES AND BEHAVIORS THAT UNDERMINE HEALING

If all of the above obstacles to healing are ruled out, you might consider whether or not the person you pray for wants to be healed. Some people are unable to let go of their sickness. This requires a major change of attitude and you can help by praying for the desire to be well.

Some people expect Jesus to heal them but they refuse to make the lifestyle changes that are necessary for their recovery. Still others expect to be healed without the help of medical experts or treatments. God speaks wisdom through health professionals but some don't listen. The healing process requires personal responsibility. You can pray that the Holy Spirit will instill the desire for wellness and motivation toward a healthy lifestyle. There is no limit to God's power to heal us when we cooperate with his grace.

You will encounter people so entrenched in conservative tradition, they shy away from the healing touch of Jesus. They may sit nervously through a healing service but never come forward for prayer. Their apprehension prevents them from opening up to healing. You can thank God for their presence, pray that they will open to the ministering of the Holy Spirit, and trust that God is touching their lives.

Obstacles to healing can become so tangled that a combination of factors works together to interfere with healing. The wall must be taken down brick by brick. A serious blockage also can result from repressed memories of sexual or physical abuse. The inner pain may be totally blocked from memory. Again, your prayers will help but professional counseling may be needed to retrieve and heal the repressed memories.

People sometimes seek relief from stress through transcendental meditation (TM), failing to realize that the mantra they chant may be the name of a Hindu god. There is only one God and he has forbidden us to worship false gods. Unlike TM, Christian meditation is focused through prayer on the one, true God.

THE POWER OF CHRIST EXPELS EVIL

Jesus gave his disciples the power to rebuke evil spirits (Lk 10:19 and Mk 16:17) and occasionally, you will discern the presence of a demonic spirit in the person for whom you pray. If you encounter a demonic spirit, don't panic. You pray for deliverance each time you pray as Jesus taught us: "...lead us not into temptation but deliver us from evil."

If you discern the presence of an evil spirit, ask Jesus to take authority over the spirit so that it cannot roam free and harm others. Invite Michael the Archangel and his legions of angels to surround and protect the person. The formula for simple deliverance prayer is: recognize the spirit, rebuke it, get on with your prayer.

A simple deliverance prayer is: "In the name of Jesus, I bind you spirit of...and I command you to leave. Lord Jesus, I ask you to take authority over this spirit so that it will harm no one. Praise you Jesus. Thank you Jesus."

At a large charismatic conference, I noticed a disruption in the front of the hall. A woman was shrieking and moaning in an outburst so loud it was drowning out the praise and worship service. As a conference prayer minister, I joined the people who were praying with her. I knew this unruly behavior was not the work of the Holy Spirit, so I quietly rebuked a spirit of disruption. Instantly, the woman became silent.

Such "familiar" spirits become attached to personality weaknesses and may be identified in people who exhibit anger, hatred, jealousy, despair, discouragement, depression, and others. Some people in ministry think they see demons in every situation. If you rely on the Holy Spirit for guidance and keep your attention properly focused on Jesus, you will maintain the proper perspective.

One prayer minister I observed repeatedly demanded that unclean spirits come out of a girl. As the girl became increasingly restless, the minister's commands intensified. Finally, the girl's eyes rolled back in her head and she began to gag. What she required was medical attention for an epileptic seizure, not deliverance. The sick girl recovered but the leader's poor discernment nearly led to disaster. People make mistakes but the Holy Spirit does not.

God uses certain people to pray in a greater way for those who have serious problems with demonic spirits. Anyone who engages in deliverance ministry requires the support of a prayer team, as well as ongoing prayers for protection. The rare problem of satanic possession falls under the authority of the local Bishop, who appoints a specially trained team to administer God's healing.

Unrepented sin holds people captive to evil, preventing them from living in the fullness of God's grace. A refusal to renounce sin interferes with God's desire to heal. Another way that people become susceptible to evil is through occult practices, which seek power and knowledge from the spiritual world, a practice God has forbidden.

A surprising number of "good" Christians are drawn into occult practices. Psychic readers, seances, ouija boards, and New Age practices are ways that people are enticed away from the Source of Life. Even when a person's intention is innocent, there is danger in such practices. The occult is seductive and those who are lured by it risk handing over control of their lives to ungodly forces. (Dt 18:10–12)

Even astrology, which on the surface may appear harmless, is a pseudoscience. Your answer to the frequently asked question, "What is your sign?" supposedly determines your personality. Horoscopes, which tell you how to live your life based on the position of the sun, stars, and planets, are just another form of divination. While astrology binds people by setting limits on their lives, we know that Jesus came to set us free.

RESTORING THE FAMILY TREE TO HEALTH

Certain complex problems respond to generational healing. Just as disease is genetically inherited, people are affected by the transgressions of their ancestors. An example is the family affected by alcoholism. Children of alcoholic parents are predisposed to having addictive personalities. This may be an inherited trait. However, children in these families also learn unhealthy patterns of problem solving and the effects of the alcoholic environment are passed on down the family line.

> ...For I, Yahweh your God, am a jealous God and I punish the father's fault in the sons, the grandsons, and the great-grandsons of those who hate me; but I show kindness to thousands of those who love me and keep my commandments. (Ex 20:5–6)

God is saying that the effects of evil are passed down through the generations, while the blessings of godly people are manifold. We inherit both the good and the bad from our ancestors. Generational healing seeks to transform and bless the negative aspects of our inheritance and this prayer is centered on forgiveness and release from bondage.

Bondage is the result of unnatural attachments that deny life and freedom by trying to exert control. Some people hold others in bondage by an unwillingness to forgive. A spouse may try to keep a partner in a stereotyped role, refusing to permit personal growth. Some parents try to control the lives of their adult children, perhaps out of fear that they will make a mistake.

There are other ways that fear controls lives. Fear of loss causes people to hold on to the terminally ill. By their unwillingness to release a loved one to God's merciful plan, people actually prolong the suffering of the dying. Fear of the unknown can also prevent a person from surrendering to the inevitable, even when death is imminent.

Difficulty in completing the grief process is another problem that is helped by prayer. People can miss their departed loved ones so much they do not release them. From the cross, Jesus told the repentant criminal, "…today you will be with me in paradise." (Lk 23:43) Jesus is the reason we can rejoice for the deceased, in spite of our natural grief for the loss of loved ones.

Demonic forces find many opportunities to penetrate people's lives. Once inside, they can contaminate a person's bloodline through sin and its effects. Since demonic spirits often attach themselves to the most vulnerable members of the family, a sensitive but innocent child may suffer the effects of evil in the family.

In his book, *Healing Your Family Tree*, Father John Hampsch, C.M.F., explains how sin can result in generational wounding. "The toxic effect of personal sin (in at least some cases) includes countless specific ailments of body, mind and spirit (1 Thes 5:23), such as cancer, arthritis, depression, anxiety, lust, perversion, rape, terrorism, alcoholism, drug addiction, and contamination by diabolic forces of evil in endless forms."[29]

When family members suffer from the consequences of sin by their parents or ancestors, the remedy is special prayers for generational healing. This involves identifying the connections in the family ancestry that will direct your prayers for healing. These problems are then presented to Jesus during the Eucharist.

The kinds of problems to look for in the family include hereditary diseases, such as alcoholism and cancer. Other clues are found in destructive behavior patterns, such as criminal behavior, untruthfulness, hatred, and anti-social conduct, which can have roots in the family history. There may be an ancestral connection in any kind of disruptive problem that is repetitive through the generations.

A pattern of mental illness is sometimes traced to ancestors. In preparing a family tree, it helps to make note of people who were unloving. They probably did not receive much love. Many families have at least one difficult relative, who especially needs prayer. The more we love and forgive, the more healing we will receive.

Generational healing can include prayers about "familial" spirits. These demonic spirits cause serious problems that repeat through the generations. For instance, a spirit of infirmity can be suspected when all of the female members of a family develop cancer. In a family with a history of suicide through the generations, you would pray about a spirit of suicide.

A family tree healing includes prayers of forgiveness for ancestors as well as prayers for healing of all the affected descendants. During a celebration of the Eucharist, the entire family is lifted up to Jesus for a severance of negative family ties to the past, for healing in the present, and for protection of future generations.

Those remembered in this prayer service include relatives who may have died "without being lovingly committed to Jesus Christ."[30] This includes miscarried babies and babies who were aborted, as well as relatives who committed suicide or suffered a sudden and traumatic death. Also, when there is unresolved grief between a living person and a deceased relative, there is probably a bondage or attachment that needs release through prayer.

Healing the family tree requires both forgiveness and collaboration with the graces poured out by God. This healing requires people to change destructive behavior and to break ties to the occult. When family skeletons are brought out into the light for forgiveness and blessing, inner doors are opened and hardened hearts may soften. This is just one more way that we can receive God's outpouring of love for us.

In 1985, prayers for family ancestors were gaining attention in the United States when we heard Father Stephen Barham speak about this approach to healing. Father Barham prayed with me about my daughter's chronic schizophrenia and on his advice, I contacted Father Hampsch. After discerning that Anne's problem was both generational and demonic, he scheduled a Mass to be said for our ancestors.

Celebration of the Eucharist is the central focus in generational healing. The compilation of a detailed family tree helped me identify family problems that might have contributed to Anne's illness. Anne and her brother John accompanied me to the Mass with Father Hampsch and in prayer, we brought our entire family to Jesus while Father Hampsch celebrated the Mass.

Afterward, Father anointed and prayed over Anne. He also prayed over John and me on behalf of other family members. Anne's healing was remarkable. Her disruptive voices, suicidal inclinations, and racing thoughts, disappeared immediately. Several days later, an evil voice returned, urging Anne to end her life. She quickly banished it by praying the simple deliverance prayer I had taught her.

In addition to Anne's healing of chronic schizophrenia, healing was experienced by both John and my husband. I personally felt that a burden had been lifted from me, and I experienced healing of a relationship within our family.

Meanwhile, my son Joe was involved in a civil lawsuit over serious injuries he had incurred as a passenger in an automobile accident. The day after our Mass for the family tree, his lawyer took the final deposition, in preparation for litigation over Joe's hip injuries. What happened was extraordinary!

Anxious to "get a burden off of his chest," one of the defendants voluntarily admitted to Joe's lawyer that he and his girlfriend had been drinking the night of the accident. He confessed that the girl had caused the accident when she ran a red light. This sworn admission of the truth resulted in a settlement in Joe's favor. God's power is unlimited.

We have seen some of the ways that prayer can overcome obstacles that interfere with healing. In serious illnesses, healing requires "soaking prayer." Parents of developmentally disabled children are encouraged to pray daily for a healing of their children's handicap. Soaking prayer is also necessary for serious mental illness.

Even when there is improvement or remission, persevere in your prayer, thanking God and asking him to continue the healing. Set aside daily prayer time to intercede for those who need constant immersion in prayer.

While generational healing focuses on healing the negative, it is important to thank God for the many blessings he has bestowed upon the family. We have inherited goodness, talents, and many good traits from ancestors. God rewards love and faithfulness with blessings down to the thousandth generation.

✝✝✝

JESUS OPENS PRISON DOORS AND FREES CAPTIVES

Sometimes people in the healing ministry agonize about "where they went wrong." Why wasn't this person healed? Why didn't I think to pray about such-and-such? It is easy to forget that the answer to prayers has nothing to do with your eloquent words. When you pray with faith for healing, God hears you.

Even when you pray silently, he knows your heart. You can pray for better discernment, but ultimately, healing does not depend on you. Healing is God's business. You are simply a channel of his love.

If your prayers do not result in healing:

1. There may be a need for spiritual healing.
2. There may be a need for inner healing.
3. Healing may be in progress but unseen.
4. There may be a need for forgiveness.
5. The person may be in a state of serious sin.
6. Consider the possibility of addictions.
7. Consider the possibility of psychosis.
8. Does the person really want to be healed?
9. Is there an unwillingness to change a lifestyle?
10. A person may have demonic attachments.
11. Consider repressed memories of abuse.
12. Ancestral bondage can block healing.
13. Has there been involvement in the occult?
14. Soaking prayer may be needed.
15. Healing may come through another.
16. Consider referral to another minister or professional.

Forgiveness and the healing of anger and hurt may be necessary before a deeper healing can occur. Anger and hurt result from: divorce; crime; injustice; terrorism; war; neglect and abuse by parents; feeling neglected and feeling misunderstood. List five other causes of hurt and anger.

Upon release from prison, Nelson Mandela said, "The worst part of imprisonment is being locked up by yourself." We imprison ourselves and others when we withhold forgiveness. With the help of Jesus, open up your prison doors and set free all the captives you are holding in a state of unforgiveness. Accept Jesus' peace and love. Feel the fresh air blowing in through the open doors.

People often find it easier to forgive others than to forgive themselves. Accept the fact that you are human and have weaknesses. Give yourself the gift of forgiveness—for your shortcomings, for your sins, for your insensitivity, for failing to live up to your own expectations. Just as others experience new life when we forgive them, the self experiences freedom and new life when we forgive ourselves.

Meditation:

Imagine yourself as a little stone. You sit on a vast plain where wind and rain erode your rough edges. This happens slowly, a drop of rain here and a burst of wind there. One day, the wind tumbles you about and tosses you into a river. In the river, you roll and slide, feeling your sides abraded by other stones. Sometimes you sink into mud. Other times, you tumble down cascading waterfalls. All of these occurrences change you. One day, you land on a grassy bank and notice your reflection in the water below. Your rough edges have been smoothed. The sun beams down upon you and your polished surface reflects the golden light.

14. Jesus Is the Resurrection and the Life

"...whoever lives and believes in me will never die." (Jn 11:26)

*R*ecent studies show that prayer has a positive effect on health, yet scientists are unable to explain how prayers to God influence healing. If medical science could explain and codify the mystery of prayer, they could prescribe it with instructions such as, "Just say two prayers, three times a day, or as often as needed to alleviate symptoms."

There is no magic in reciting the words of prayers. The faith behind the prayers is what matters. When we pray, we trust in God's love for us and in his faithfulness to his promises. While we would like to know in advance how prayers will be answered, it is not important for us to know. Human nature is weak. We might abandon our prayers if we disagreed with the outcome he had planned.

ACCEPT THE WISDOM OF THE HEALER

I want everyone I pray for to be healed. I pray for miracles. I want to see lives transformed. I long for souls to be set on fire with love for Jesus. Meanwhile, God gently reminds me that the healing I want is not necessarily the healing he intends.

Through years of praying for others, I have learned to accept the wisdom of the Healer. People always receive healing at some level when we pray. God is full of surprises and his reasons for granting, or not granting, a physical healing may be

149

very complex. The healing ministry takes you deep into the mystery of God.

At no time is the mystery deeper than when death is the answer to your prayers. In the Emergency Room of a busy hospital, I listened as a nurse puzzled over the paradoxical situation around him. He and other members of the ER team were fighting to save lives. Nine patients were desperately clinging to life, but a tenth patient had tried to end his. Why is life so precious to some and not to others?

Jesus asked a sick man lying by the Pool of Bethesda, "Do you want to be well again?" (Jn 5:6) When I pray for someone who is terminally ill, I ask how they want me to pray. Not everyone wants to be physically healed.

One man I prayed with was healed of a cancerous brain tumor, a fact his doctor confirmed. In spite of his cure, he refused to believe the cancer was gone and he constantly complained of pain. Later, I learned that he was so addicted to pain medication, the drugs were causing phantom pain similar to that caused by the cancer. This man could not accept a miracle. Ironically, his cancer eventually returned.

> We are quite confident that if we ask him for anything, and it is in accordance with his will, he will hear us; and, knowing that whatever we may ask, he hears us, we know that we have already been granted what we asked of him.
>
> (1 Jn 5:14–15)

YOUR WILL BE DONE, LORD

It is important to pray in accordance with the will of God. Just a short time after my own miraculous healing, I visited a family friend who was seriously ill. I took along my son Patrick, on whom I had been practicing my prayers for healing. Though new to this ministry, I was hopeful that I could pray with Randall and bring him the kind of healing I had received.

The tall, handsome man I remembered was now bent with pain from his cancerous liver. His thin hair was gray and his face looked older than it should have. The sight of this sick man filled my heart with compassion as he told us about his futile attempts to find a cure. When I asked if he believed in God, he showed me his well-worn Bible. Then he opened his life and laid scenes of it before us.

Toward the end of our visit, I sat next to Randall with my arm around his frail shoulders and listened as he shared his recurring dream. Randall traveled through a dark tunnel, focusing on a pinpoint of light in the distance. His passengers had stepped out of the car, leaving him to proceed alone. At last, he emerged at the far end of the tunnel into a brilliant light. The scene was breathtaking. He overlooked a beach where he saw Jesus and all of the saints, dressed in the most beautiful colors imaginable.

Randall was sobbing, his face drenched with tears. "If only I could know what that dream means. I have that same dream over and over again! It is so beautiful and it always makes me cry. Can you tell me what it means, Pat?"

For a moment, I was silent. How could I explain that he was going to die? Finally, I choked back my own tears and said, "You know what the dream means, Randall. The meaning is within you." His pain was worsening and it was time for his medication. We had to leave.

I could not stop my tears as we drove away. "He's going to die, Patrick," I cried. "He's going to die and I didn't even pray for his healing. I wanted to pray over him and I couldn't do it, because I know he will die soon. I just didn't know what to do."

"Mom," Patrick said, his thirteen-year-old voice filled with wisdom and insight, "you weren't supposed to ask God to heal his cancer. If you were, you would have done it." I knew he was right. Later, Father John McGregor confirmed what Patrick had said. He told me the Lord would always lead me. I would know when Jesus wanted me to pray for healing. He would give me a sense of certainty.

UNDERSTANDING SPECIAL NEEDS OF THE DYING

Often, people have unfinished business that prevents them from yielding to death. Through your sensitive listening and discernment, you can help the dying lay to rest their concerns about the living. Relieved of their anxiety, they are then in a better disposition either to receive healing or to surrender to the final call of Jesus.

A frail woman I visited was on the precipice of death. Her skin was tightly stretched over her bones and her abdomen was grossly swollen by a tumor. The slightest movement caused her pain. I could feel the intensity of her family gathered around her bed. They wanted a miracle. I asked the woman, "What would you like me to pray about?" She longed for healing of her damaged relationship with her mother and she wanted prayers for her family. I prayed accordingly, asking also for a physical healing if that was God's will. She died peacefully within a week.

At times, you can be easily misled by false signs that seem to indicate healing. When one young woman came to me for prayer, she was doubled over like a little old lady. The lines in her face revealed the intensity of her pain. We discovered that I could alleviate her pain by praying with my hand on her back where the hurt was most severe. Jesus was ministering his touch through mine.

After prayers for healing, her face was radiant with peace. I felt a strong presence of love each time I prayed for her and we noticed a dramatic reduction in the size of her tumor. A miracle, however, was not the answer to our prayers. Within a short time, a new eruption of tumors made it clear to me that her disease was malicious and unrelenting. She endured tremendous suffering before she closed her eyes for the last time.

From the human viewpoint, this young woman's death saddened me. We stormed heaven with prayers for a miracle, but Jesus had a different plan. The love we felt each time we prayed together was the presence of Jesus. Released from her earthly suffering, she now abides in his presence. Death is a victory for those who know Jesus because he has promised us a full reward with his Father in heaven. This is the homecoming for which the soul was created.

Ruth, a woman with advanced cancer, had already outlived her doctor's expectations. Based on his examination and her worsening symptoms, he estimated that she had only a few months to live. I prayed that she would have a peaceful and painfree death. Meanwhile, she received prayers from another minister of healing.

Her symptoms continued to worsen and Ruth decided to risk major surgery. In spite of her age and the fact that she suffered a minor stroke prior to the surgery, she survived without the expected complications. Her doctor was amazed. Her cancer was in remission.

Why does Jesus call home a young woman with her whole life ahead of her, and extend the life of an 86-year-old woman? Which of these people received the better healing? Why did one person pray over Ruth for a miracle, while I prayed for her peaceful death? I do not know the answers, but I am confident that my prayers will be answered too.

HEALING WITH THE BREAD OF LIFE AND
ORDINARY LOVE

I bring the Eucharist to one elderly woman who has had several close brushes with death. After a recent illness, she returned to her retirement home with a poor appetite. It was painful to watch this frail woman growing weaker as she refused to eat. When a relative mentioned that breakfast was the woman's favorite meal, a cook prepared a ham-and-egg sandwich. The woman ate every morsel and crumb and her appetite continued to improve. The cook was visibly touched to see the healing power of her simple sandwich.

Jesus, who heals through his presence in the Eucharist, also heals through human love and encouragement. That simple ham-and-egg sandwich was Eucharist. I mean no irreverence by the comparison. The sandwich was nourishment for the spirit as well for the body. It was prepared with love, and it gave the woman a burst of life and strength.

One woman whose cancer was widespread was unable to eat solid food. While she badly needed physical healing, her desire for a peanut butter sandwich seemed foremost on her mind. I promised to make one if her doctor approved, and he did. Maria was so happy when I delivered the sandwich I had prepared in the hospital snack room. I tiptoed out so she could enjoy her feast in privacy. Before her death a week later, she left me this message: "That was the best peanut butter sandwich I ever tasted!"

This then is what we bring when we pray. We bring the love of the living Christ, his compassion, and his hope. We bring it in the form of listening hearts, healing hands, faith-filled prayers, anointing with oil, compassion for his little ones, and sometimes with Eucharist. We may even bring his love in ham-and-egg or peanut butter sandwiches.

Lives are touched by God's love when friends pray for one another and bear each others' burdens. In one home for the elderly, I have seen residents pat one another on the shoulder when they pass by. In response, those who receive the love-pats reach up and squeeze the hands that touched them. Love is happening and love is healing.

When you minister to the sick, you are invited into their pain and suffering. At times, that suffering will end in death and you may be the one chosen by God to prepare someone to meet Jesus. Jesus may use your presence to help a family in denial reach an acceptance of impending death. Also, you will help people overcome their grief through your prayer ministry.

Grief must run its natural course. When you pray with others about prolonged and unnatural grief, you may uncover unresolved issues with the deceased. There might be self-blame for a person's death. Some may hold others responsible for a loved one's death. Still others will be angry with the deceased for leaving them. These sensitive areas must be approached prayerfully.

Through prayer you can help people release loved ones into the arms of Jesus. Just like Simon of Cyrene, who in a spirit of love helped Jesus carry his cross, you can help others carry theirs. By your companionship, you can help them to celebrate good memories of their loved ones. Sometimes, just talking about a deceased person's qualities and goodness can help the grief-stricken release loved ones. Then God can expedite their grief process.

The occasion of death brings out the worst, as well as the best, in families. Bickering and disagreements sometimes erupt and add to family grief. Your prayers can be directed at helping them focus on the spiritual blessings, rather than on their personal feelings of sadness and their unfulfilled expectations.

Jesus was sold out by Judas for thirty silver coins. As soon as he was crucified, Roman soldiers divided his clothing and gambled to see who would claim his tunic. Similarly, family members sometimes react to death by quarreling over the deceased's worldly possessions. The best remembrances of loved ones are memories of the love and the happiness they shared with you. Material things grow old and shabby but good memories last forever.

Death brings us face to face with our own mortality. Some people are so fearful of death, they deny the inevitable. While physical death is a natural consequence of life, it does not quench the soul, which is supernatural and immortal. We overcome fear of death by placing it in its proper perspective. Death is a normal life process and it provides an opportunity for the great spiritual homecoming of the soul.

Frequently, we take our loved ones for granted. We may postpone asking forgiveness when it is needed, and we sometimes behave as though we have forever to express our love and gratitude. It is imperative to say the important things that loved ones need to hear while they are living.

THERE IS A TIME FOR LETTING GO

My father died quite suddenly. Initially he appeared to have the flu, but within a few hours he was in septic shock. He was already semi-conscious when we reached the hospital in the middle of the night. I called at once for a priest, who administered the Sacrament of the Sick.

My dad could hear our voices, but his eyes were glazed over and unseeing. A ventilator helped his breathing but he was restless. He thrashed around and tried to identify whose voice it was that said, "Tom, I hope you make it but if you die tonight, you will go straight to heaven. All your sins are forgiven." Comforted by the chaplain's words, my dad immediately lapsed into a deep and peaceful sleep. He died with dignity a few hours later.

While it was difficult to lose my father, I am grateful that we had grown very close in the years just prior to his death. As I stood by his bed in intensive care, there was only time to say, "I love you, Daddy." It was enough. It was time to let go.

There is a time for letting go. When we hold on too tightly to our loved ones, they must feel like they are the rope in a tug-of-war, with God pulling on one end and the family pulling on the other. It is as important to be sensitive to the needs of the dying as it is to be understanding of the needs of the sick.

One man in the final stages of cancer was suffering from depression. An agnostic most of his life, he had no faith in God to sustain him. After speaking with his wife, I began praying for healing at every level. Meanwhile, she told her husband about her experience of a loving God. This man opened his heart to Jesus and began praying with his wife. Shortly after his spiritual healing, he died in the embrace of Jesus.

I believe God so desires our company, he gives each one countless opportunities to choose life with him in heaven. In the parable of the workers in the vineyard, Jesus taught that the late-arriving workers are treated as well as those who work the entire day.

When we minister to the dying, it is beneficial to pray they will experience the love and peace of Jesus in their final moments. One way we help them know that peace is by praying about their worldly concerns. People experience tremendous relief when they have clarified their decisions.

When I visited Alicia in the hospital, I asked what she would like to pray about. Alicia wanted peace and clear thinking so that she could make a decision. "Without a certain procedure," she said, "I will die." I asked Jesus to hold Alicia and touch all the hidden places where she hurt. I also prayed for his peace and love to fill her so that she could make the best decision.

When I returned two weeks later, Alicia had made her choice. She was dying. I could feel the love and peace in her room as I sat quietly and prayed, feeling privileged to share in her final moments. When Alicia opened her eyes, she spoke with urgency, "I need to see my children!" Death was near and this was a dramatic change of heart. I left so she could conserve her strength for her children.

Alicia had devoted her energies to helping others with cancer. She was dedicated to educating people and to helping them combat and survive the disease. While I knew she would be missed, it was comforting to know that she died in the peace of Christ, who promised:

> I am the resurrection and the life.
> If anyone believes in me, even though he dies he will live,
> and whoever lives and believes in me
> will never die.
> Do you believe this? (Jn 11:25–26)

A good friend of my youth was confident in Jesus' promise and he seemed comfortable about the homecoming that awaited him. In a letter that he dictated from his deathbed, Father Felix Penna, S.D.B., wrote: "I am in the hands of God and eager to do His Holy Will. I have enjoyed and treasured your friendship…I will remember you there where no other cares, nor time, nor occupations will interfere with Love. Goodbye. I shall await you in heaven. Do not fail me."

Jesus himself is asking us not to fail him. He awaits our arrival and looks forward to spending eternity with us.

THE HOMECOMING FOR WHICH THE SOUL WAS CREATED

As Christians, we know that Jesus has earned for us eternal life in his kingdom. Yet, we cling desperately to life, postponing our final reward. Some that you pray for will die and you will experience grief. You will also encounter your own mortality. Once you confront the reality of death, it loses its power to frighten you.

Read the accounts of Jesus' death and resurrection as told by the four evangelists. What does scripture teach about ministering to the dying and to the grief-stricken?

Read John 14:1–4. What did Jesus mean when he said: "You know the way to the place where I am going."

At a grief workshop, participants were told to imagine that they had only a few days to live. They were directed to go home and carefully examine their priorities. One oncology nurse spent the entire weekend cleaning out closets so that she would not be remembered as disorganized.

When you are really terminally ill, your priorities change. My top priority was to achieve a deeper relationship with God. My second priority was to spend meaningful time with family members and with my friends. I celebrated life with them, hoping they would remember me fully alive. Living is more important than organizing.

Review your priorities from time to time and notice whether or not they are changing. By living your life more consciously, you can create good memories for yourself and for your loved ones.

Imagine that you have only twenty-four hours to live. How will you spend your final hours? What do you need to tell people? Write it down.

Is there a departed loved one whom you miss terribly? What would you like to tell that loved one? Write down your thoughts in a letter and ask Jesus to deliver the message.

Write your own obituary. Briefly emphasize the important contributions that you have made. Try to express what you think family and friends would say about you.

You have been invited to write a brief eulogy to be read at your own funeral. How do you want to be remembered?

When you or those you pray for are fearful about death, pray on this scripture:

> ...know that I am with you always; yes, to the end of time.
> (Mt 28:20)

15. Healing the World

"He was in the world…and the world did not know him." (Jn 1:10)

*I*n his Sermon on the Mount, Jesus announced his plan for his little ones, a plan of action to be carried out by his followers. The disciples who work with Jesus are recognized by attributes of gentleness, moral righteousness, mercy, purity of heart, poverty of spirit, and peacemaking. Jesus says that faith is essential, but much more is expected of those who will join him in the kingdom.

Heaven is your destination but your ticket to heaven is your response to the Beatitudes. This is not a popular idea. Self-centeredness can easily erode the social conscience. In the world, we are surrounded by values of money and power, values which contradict the Beatitudes. The little ones are suffering and when one segment of humanity suffers, we all suffer.

BE LITTLE!

The problems of God's little ones are our problems and it is through godly values, rather than worldly ones, that we can help. While it is honorable to donate money to worthy causes, financial support is not enough. Material wealth will never fill the void that is created each time human dignity is compromised. Economic assistance cannot atone for acts that destroy the human spirit, acts such as the violation of human rights or the damage caused by war and violence.

Jesus was not on the side of money and power. Neither was he complacent. If you have grown comfortable in your faith and beliefs, be careful. Jesus comforts us but he also expects us to extend his comfort to others. He expects us to set aside our complacency and do something.

He who made us in his image wants us to respect all of his creations. Jesus did not say, "Be powerful." He did not say, "Be comfortable." He did not say, "Be wealthy." He did not say, "Belittle." He said, "Be little."

Suffering is all around us. Problems in the world are enormous and we often feel helpless over the plight of the little ones. Yet, idealistic as it may seem, the only hope for a better world is in living Christ's Beatitudes. How can you possibly heal the world when you have not healed the people in your own family, let alone in your neighborhood? The truth is that you can make a significant difference.

START AN AVALANCHE OF HEALING

You can begin to heal the world one person at a time. When you heal one person and bring them into deeper relationship with Jesus, that person can bring the same healing to another. And once you have touched one person with the healing power of Jesus, you can reach out to another. Just think of the dynamics that will result.

I am neither a mathematician nor a statistician, but I know that this one-on-one healing can become an avalanche. The human race needs healing at the most basic levels so that we can begin to live as God's people. Healing can begin between you and those who are closest to your life. It will be marked by acceptance and forgiveness, and by the elimination of feuding and backbiting. When you restore peace to your family, look to your wider family in the neighborhood, at church, and in the workplace.

Imagine a world in which love is the driving force! Imagine a neighborhood where everyone really cares about the neighbors! Imagine a country governed by love rather than politics, by compassion rather than money or power! Imagine a world in which there is no division among races. Imagine a world in which everyone sees the beauty of each one's inner spirit, and recognizes the God who dwells within. Imagine a world being cured of bigotry, hate, greed, self-centeredness, and disrespect for each human's dignity.

HEALING DISUNITY IN GOD'S FAMILY

Spiritual leaders are taking the lead in world healing by their actions to resolve differences that cause disunity in God's family. In 1995, some leaders repented their churches' actions of the past. The Evangelical Lutheran Church apologized for Martin Luther's anti-Semitism, while Pope John Paul II acknowledged failure by the Roman Catholic Church to support human rights within totalitarian governments. As some Pentecostal churches were adopting new interracial leadership roles, Southern Baptists were apologizing for the early pro-slavery attitude of their church.[31]

In addition to peacemaking efforts among church bodies, there has been a wave of repentance between various ethnic and nationality groups. It appears that a new movement of the Holy Spirit is at work to heal the divisions in God's church.

JESUS AND CHILDREN, OUR HOPE FOR THE FUTURE

In a hopeful message celebrating the 1996 World Day of Peace, Pope John Paul II appealed to people everywhere to help create an environment of peace for today's children. Young people are the hope of the future for a better world, and the first lessons of peace are learned in the family. "Peace," he says, "is a gift of God; but men and women must first accept this gift in order to build a peaceful world. People can do this only if they have a childlike simplicity of heart."[32]

In a subsequent message, the Holy Father stressed his optimism that "humanity's path will be illuminated by the light of the One who, in coming into this world, became our travelling companion...."[33] The Pontiff's goal for the millennium is to unify Christians and to lead people to a greater consciousness toward God's little ones.

John Paul II has entreated youth to serve the poor, the hungry, the homeless, the lonely, and the ill. He has also urged young people to "stand up for life" by taking a stand against abortion, pornography, euthanasia and assisted suicide, while standing for marriage, family life, and purity.[34] This challenge, which echoes the Sermon on the Mount, recognizes the contribution that can be made by young people whose values are still in the formative stage.

One California school strives to improve character development with a program based on Gene Bedley's book *Values in Action*. Students are taught values of: respect, integrity, compassion, fortitude, responsibility, resilience, and cooperation. These lessons are taught in the classroom and emphasized on the playground, with older students acting as mentors for younger children. After only one year, the program was credited with improved academic attention, better attendance, and fewer discipline problems.[35]

Programs that reinforce good values and respect for others improve the prospects for a peaceful world. The movement toward peace and love will be further hastened when each one of us accepts and embraces one another in a true spirit of love. This results when we focus on our similarities, rather than on the differences which separate God's people. It is that simple. Look around you. God's healing touch is needed everywhere. Where will you begin?

The first step toward healing the world is awareness. There is no shortage of work, only a shortage of laborers in the vineyard. There are numerous ways to contribute. You can begin close to home in an area that utilizes the special gifts of your unique personality and talents.

One woman with a special interest in combatting alcohol and drug abuse started a small prayer group that meets for an hour every week. These "prayer warriors" have seen impressive results from their faithful prayers about alcohol and drug problems in their community. In addition, their prayers have been extended to include the sick and needy in their parish.

One church has a successful prayer chain ministry. The first person on the list receives notification of a prayer request and calls two more people. These two each call two more, until everyone on the list is notified. In this way, a lot of people quickly become involved whenever prayers are needed.

A charismatic prayer group devotes a portion of their weekly meeting to praying about the requests they have received. In addition to praying for these intentions, their prayers are an ongoing source of strength to their church leadership and membership. Another intercessory prayer group paired their members with the people in need of prayers. As a beneficiary of their prayer ministry when I had cancer, I felt blessed by the love and concern from my prayer partner's cheery notes and encouragement.

One police officer, using his knowledge of gang activities, became involved by working with youth groups. It is easier to steer young people in a positive direction than it is to rescue them from a negative environment. Prevention pays huge rewards.

Good citizens are informed about local, national, and global issues and vote responsibly, with a moral conscience. One busy executive, whose travel schedule prevents his personal involvement in the community, discovered a simple way to make a difference. He voices his concerns about abortion and other moral issues by writing letters. Informed about his views, his Congressional representatives notify him about pending legislation on these issues.

After his retirement from business, one man found satisfaction by making audio recordings of books for the blind. He also contributes his skills by writing letters on behalf of Amnesty International, a group dedicated to the protection of human rights throughout the world.

A woman who is unable to work because of job-related disabilities found the niche where she can make a difference. Throughout each day, she prays constantly for the needs of others. Since pain and suffering are her personal cross, her experiences have deepened her compassion for others in pain. Each time she visits the doctor, she tries to reach out to at least one other person who needs prayer.

YOU CAN HEAL THE WORLD!

Your response to the Beatitudes can find many expressions. Prayer is the most obvious way to help others. Everyone can pray, regardless of circumstances or occupations. In addition to praying for family and friends, you can extend your reach to include world issues, one at a time. Perhaps you could spend a month praying about problems of the elderly. The next month, you could pray for victims of crime.

Another approach is to target a different issue each day. A calendar with space to write each day's intention will help you remember your commitment.

Your intercessory prayer might begin with your immediate family, ancestors, neighbors, your church, your community, the workplace, schools, and the sick and needy in your area. You can include those who do not know God and those who are alienated from him. Children, who represent hope for the future, especially need prayers.

Next you could focus on victims: aborted babies, their parents, crime victims, the abused, the forgotten elderly, abandoned youth, and lonely people everywhere.

You can pray for all the needy people who cross your path, as well as the less visible needy: the homeless, the unemployed, drug addicts, sex addicts, gambling addicts, satanists, alcoholics, the mentally ill, the physically handicapped, homosexuals, the developmentally disadvantaged, AIDS patients, and prostitutes.

Others who desperately need the light of Christ are those caught up in violent activities, including: abusers, molesters, rapists, terrorists, criminals, gang members, and the mafia. Prayers for children to learn non-violent behavior can also lead to a more peaceful world.

Prayers for wisdom and guidance are needed by government leaders, legislative bodies, judges, religious leaders, and all those who minister God's word. You can include law enforcement officers, military personnel, teachers, social workers, and all those who strive to make the world a just and peaceful place.

There is a need to pray for scientific breakthroughs in the field of medicine. Your prayers can embrace those who suffer from specific diseases, as well as their doctors, nurses, and caregivers who constantly "lay hands on the sick."

Prayers for global peace can be directed toward world concerns, countries at war, the oppression of human rights, those who suffer from hunger and famine, victims of natural disasters,

and the division among God's people. You can also pray for
future generations, for a healing of the environment, and for
total world peace.

Aside from prayers, the next step in healing the world
requires your action. With your new awareness of God's little
ones and your preparedness to be the presence of Christ in the
world, you will hear the call to become personally involved
when you see a need. When you minister to the little ones, you
will shine in the world "like a lamp in the dark." (Ps 112:4)

✝ ✝ ✝

WELL DONE, LITTLE ONE

Jesus has delegated the task of saving the world to his disciples. He challenges us to love everyone, to put our love into action, and to spread the Good News.

Read Isaiah 58. How will you free the oppressed, share your bread, shelter the homeless, clothe the naked, and above all, love? Will you be a light in the darkness?

> ...your light must shine in the sight of men, so that, seeing your good works, they may give the praise to your Father in heaven. (Mt 5:16)

> The question is world peace. The answer is:
> *Awareness—Prayerfulness—Preparedness—Action*

Even though the challenge is great, you do not have to work alone. Jesus goes with you every step of the way. Your little beacon of light is but a tiny reflection of his brightness.

> ...God is light; there is no darkness in him at all. (1 Jn 1:5)

As you embark on your journey of ministering to the little ones so dear to the heart of Jesus, you have the consolation of his Holy Spirit to comfort and guide you. The journey may be long and difficult, but the rewards Jesus has promised sustain you. Close your eyes and imagine yourself at the end of your travels. At last, you sit down to rest and to reflect on where you have been.

Meditation:
You are sitting in a beautiful garden. It is pleasant, neither hot nor cold, and a gentle breeze freshens the air. It is the end of a long day but there is no darkness. In the bright sky overhead, you see Jesus seated upon a white cloud descending toward you. He speaks: "Well done, faithful servant. You have loved well. Come! Receive your reward." Joyfully, you hang up your work gloves and walk into the embrace of Jesus.

Notes

A Note to the Reader

1. *Cancer Facts & Figures 1995;* American Cancer Society, Inc. (figures stated in round numbers).

Chapter 1.

2. It is important to realize that no two incidents of cancer are the same. While my disease was untreatable, it would be wrong to conclude that another person with the same or similar symptoms has the same prognosis. Such a diagnosis can only be made by specialists. Furthermore, medical science continues to make great strides in the treatment of illnesses that were once considered hopeless. Readers are encouraged to believe in and experience the healing love of Jesus, who gives us hope even when the world does not.

Chapter 2.

3. In architecture, the keystone is the wedge-shaped stone at the top and center of an arch. The support of all the other stones in the arch is dependent upon the keystone.

Chapter 3.

4. Gerard Manley Hopkins, "That Nature is a Heraclitean Fire and of the Comfort of the Resurrection," *Poems,* ed. W. H. Gardner (New York: Penguin Books, 1953, reprinted 1982), pp. 65–66.
5. Jean Vanier is a Catholic layman who founded L'Arche homes for the mentally handicapped in 22 countries throughout the world.
6. University of San Diego, June 24–29, 1990, directed by Jean Vanier and Rev. Jim O'Donnell. Coordinated by Betty Britschgi, Special Religious Education Consultant under the auspices of Office of Catechetical Ministry, Diocese of San Diego, California.
7. Father Jim O'Donnell, diocesan priest in the Diocese of Cleveland, was the North American Coordinator for Faith and Sharing Retreats.

8. John F. Winters is founder/Executive Director of GOAL, INC.

9. Jean Vanier.

10. Words on a poster.

Chapter 4.

11. Kahlil Gibran, *The Wisdom of Gibran*, ed. by Joseph Sheban (New York: Carol Publishing Group, Citadel Press, 1971).

12. Source unknown. Story may have been inspired by a similar story told by the Persian poet and writer, Sadi. "A Rose in a Tuft of Grass," excerpted by Claire Powell in *The Meaning of Flowers* (Boulder, CO: Shambhala, 1979), p. 119.

13. Merlin Carothers, *Prison to Praise* (Foundation of Praise, Escondido, CA: 1970, 1992).

14. Catherine Marshall, *Something More* (New York: Avon Books,1974), pp. 1–24 and 29–30.

15. "High-Tech Prayers; Faxes to God," *Family Circle* (February 1, 1994) p. 8.

Chapter 5.

16. *Great People of the Bible and How They Lived* (NY: Reader's Digest Association, Inc., 1974), pp. 340-343.

17. Norman Cousins, *Anatomy of An Illness* (Toronto, NY, and London: Bantam Books, 1981; by arrangement with W.W. Norton & Co. 1979), pp. 34 & 154.

18. Robert Ornstein, Ph.D., and David Sobel, M.D., *Healthy Pleasures* (MA, NY, CA: Addison-Wesley Publishing Company, 1989), pp. 216–217.

19. George Macdonald: *Sir Gibbie,* chapter 23, cited in *George Macdonald: An Anthology,* ed. C.S. Lewis (New York: Dolphin Books 1962, Doubleday & Company, Inc., 1947), p. 139, no. 319.

20. Archaic definition for *fear; Webster's Seventh New Collegiate Dictionary* (MA: G. & C. Merriam Company, 1972).

Chapter 7.

21. Brother Daniel F. Stramara, O.S.B., "Signs and Wonders: God Among Us!" (Pecos, NM: Dove Publications), Leaflet #66.

Chapter 8.

22. *Webster's Seventh New Collegiate Dictionary.*
23. William Saroyan, "Wealth as a State of Mind," *Family Circle* (May 1974), p. 34.

Chapter 10.

24. Blessed oil, which is different from sacramental oil, is olive oil blessed by a priest or bishop for use by the laity. The blessing, from the old *Roman Ritual,* can be found in *Healing the Dying,* p. 81. (see Resources)

Chapter 11.

25. Henri Daniel-Rops, *Daily Life in the Time of Jesus* (Ann Arbor, MI: Servant Books), p. 357.
26. Anthony de Mello, S.J., *Sadhana: a Way to God, Christian Exercises in Eastern Form,* Exercise 20 (St. Louis, MO: The Institute of Jesuit Sources, 1978), p. 69.

Chapter 12.

27. Charles L. Whitfield, M.D., *Healing the Child Within,* p. 2. (see Resources)
28. Robert Lee Hotz, "Detective Work That Leaves No Footprints," *Los Angeles Times,* November 16, 1995, page 1.

Chapter 13.

29. John H. Hampsch, C.M.F., *Healing Your Family Tree* (WA: Performance Press, 1986), Foreword.
30. Dr. Kenneth McAll, *Healing the Family Tree,* p. 52.

Chapter 15.

31. "Joining the Rush to Repent" by John Dart, *Los Angeles Times,* June 19, 1995, p. 1.
32. "Let Us Give Children a Future of Peace" (Message of His Holiness Pope John Paul II for the Celebration of the World Day of Peace; 1 January 1996).
33. Address of the Holy Father Privato on the occasion of the Exchange

of Greetings with the Diplomatic Corps accredited to the Holy See (Saturday, 13 January 1996).

34. "Pope Offers Vision of Church for Millennium" by John J. Goldman and Larry B. Stammer, *Los Angeles Times*, October 8, 1995, p. 1.
35. "School Spells Out a Curriculum of Respect and Values" by Paul H. Johnson, *Los Angeles Times*, February 7, 1996, p. B-2

Suggested Reading

Catechism of the Catholic Church. New York, London, Toronto, Sydney, Auckland: Doubleday, 1995.

Christopher News Notes, 12 East 48th St., New York, NY 10017. Free news notes. Rev. James Keller, M.M. founded The Christophers with the motto, "It's better to light one candle than to curse the darkness."

de Mello, Anthony, S.J., *Sadhana a Way to God: Christian Exercises in Eastern Form.* St. Louis, MO: The Institute of Jesuit Sources, 1978.

Dove Publications, Pecos, New Mexico 87552. Publications on healing, the charismatic renewal, and related topics.

Hampsch, John H., C.M.F., *Healing Your Family Tree,* and other publications and teaching tapes. Claretian Tape Ministry, P.O. Box 19100, Los Angeles, CA 90019-0100.

Kelsey, Morton T., *The Christian and the Supernatural.* Minneapolis, MN: Augsburg Publishing House, 1976.

Kelsey, Morton T., *Healing and Christianity.* New York, Hagerstown, San Francisco, and London: Harper & Row, Publishers, 1973 and 1976.

Linn, Mary Jane, C.S.J., Linn, Dennis, S.J., and Linn, Matthew, S.J., *Healing the Dying.* New York/Mahwah, NJ: Paulist Press, 1979.

Linn, Matthew, S.J., and Linn, Dennis, S.J., *Healing of Memories.* New York/Mahwah, NJ: Paulist Press, 1974.

Linn, Matthew, S.J., Linn, Dennis, S.J., and Fabricant, Sheila, *Healing the Greatest Hurt.* New York/Mahwah, NJ: Paulist Press, 1985.

MacNutt, Francis, O.P., *Healing.* Notre Dame, IN: Ave Maria Press, 1974, 1979, revised 1988.

MacNutt, Francis, O.P., *The Power to Heal.* Notre Dame, IN: Ave Maria Press, 1977.

McAll, Kenneth, *Healing the Family Tree.* London: Sheldon Press, 1982.

Nouwen, Henri J.M., *The Wounded Healer.* New York: Image Books, A Division of Doubleday & Co., Inc., 1972, 1979.

Sanford, Agnes, *The Healing Gifts of the Spirit.* Philadelphia and New York: A Holman Book, J. B. Lippincott Co., 1966. Also, San Francisco: Harper San Francisco, 1984.

Sanford, Agnes, *The Healing Light.* Plainfield, NJ: Logos International, Macalester Park Publishing Co., 1947, 1972, 1976. Also, New York: Ballantine Books, Inc., 1983.

Schubert, Linda, *Miracle Hour.* 1991. (Prayer booklet) P.O. Box 4034, Santa Clara, CA 95056.

Shlemon, Barbara Leahy, *Healing the Hidden Self.* Notre Dame, IN: Ave Maria Press, 1982, 1987.

Vanier, Jean, *The Broken Body: Journey to Wholeness.* New York/Mahwah, NJ: Paulist Press, 1988.

Vanier, Jean, *Jesus the Gift of Love.* New York: Crossroad Publishing Co., 1994.

Whitfield, Charles L., M.D., *Healing the Child Within.* Deerfield Beach, FL: Health Communications, Inc., 1987, 1989.

Resources

Catholic Answers, P.O. Box 17490, San Diego, CA 92177. (619) 541-1131. A resource for answers to questions concerning apologetics.

Faith & Light:
International Coordinator:
Maureen O'Reilly, 1428 Elm, Dearborn, MI 48124

National Coordinators:
U.S.A. East:
Sister Florita Rodman, 738 Court St., Brockton, MA 02402
U.S.A. West:
John and Diane Griffin, 2243 Palm Dr., Colorado Springs, CO 80918

Zone Coordinators:
Frank and Pat Dani,
2354 E. Briarhurst Dr.,
Highlands Ranch, CO 80126

International ecumenical association of mentally handicapped people, their families and friends; founded by Jean Vanier and Marie Helénè Mathieu.

Faith & Sharing Retreats:
Coordinator:
Maggie Conrad, Little Brothers and Sisters of the Eucharist, 2182 E. 35th St, Cleveland, OH 44115-3039
Retreats share the gospel message and the spirit of the Beatitudes, as taught by Jean Vanier.

GOAL, INC. (Get Out and Live!):

John F. Winters, Executive Director, 14040 N.E. 11th Avenue, North Miami, FL 33161-3302. (305) 895-6377.
Non-profit organization which encourages the homebound handicapped to develop job skills and to become involved in the community.

International Catholic Charismatic Renewal Office
Palazzo Del Cancelleria 00120, Vatican City.

L'Arche Communities for the Mentally Handicapped:
Zone Coordinator for Western Canada and the United States:
Marni Davis, 7401 Sussex Avenue, Burnaby, B.C. Canada
V5J 3V6.
Telephone: (604) 438-6883; Fax: (604) 435-9560

Zone Coordinator for Eastern Canada (Ontario, Quebec &
Maritimes):
Jean-Christophe Pascal, c/o L'Arche Montreal, 6646 Boulevard
Monk, Montreal, Quebec H4E 3J1.
Telephone: (514) 768-5422; Fax: (514) 278-9493

National Service Committee, Catholic Charismatic Renewal of the
United States, Inc., P.O. Box 628, Locust Grove, VA 22508-0628,
(703) 972-0225. Publishes *Leaders Directory* of Catholic Charismatic
Prayer Groups in the United States. For information on Leadership Programs: 1-800-338-2445.